KYIV 2022

Russia's disastrous invasion of Ukraine

MARK GALEOTTI

OSPREY PUBLISHING
Bloomsbury Publishing Plc

Kemp House, Chawley Park, Cumnor Hill, Oxford OX2 9PH, UK
Bloomsbury Publishing Ireland Limited,
29 Earlsfort Terrace, Dublin 2, D02 AY28, Ireland
1385 Broadway, 5th Floor, New York, NY 10018, USA
E-mail: info@ospreypublishing.com
www.ospreypublishing.com

OSPREY is a trademark of Osprey Publishing Ltd

First published in Great Britain in 2026

ISBN: PB 9781472869524; eBook: 9781472869517;
ePDF: 9781472869548; XML: 9781472869531

26 27 28 29 30 10 9 8 7 6 5 4 3 2 1

Maps by www.bounford.com
3D BEV by Alan Gilliard
Index by Richard Munro
Typeset by PDQ Digital Media Solutions, Bungay, UK
Printed by Repro India Ltd

Title page caption: Ukrainian soldiers on the collapsed bridge at Irpin aim
for a suspected Russian observation drone. (Getty)

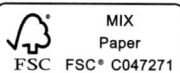

Author's Note
Translating from foreign alphabets always poses challenges. I have chosen
to transliterate names as they are pronounced, and have also ignored the
diacritical 'soft' and 'hard' signs found in the original Cyrillic. The only
exceptions are names that have acquired common forms in English – for
example, I use the spelling 'Chernobyl' rather than the correct Ukrainian
form 'Chornobyl.' There are, after all, also political minefields to be
traversed. Ukrainian words, names, and places are transliterated
Ukrainian-style, while their Russian counterparts likewise are transliterated
accordingly. For names, the individuals' preferred forms are used.

Abbreviations used in this text:

AA	anti-air
AFV	armoured fighting vehicle
APC	armoured personnel carrier
AT	antitank
Bde	Brigade
Bn	Battalion
BTG	Battalion Tactical Group
Bty	Battery
Col.	Colonel
Coy	Company
Div	Division
DNR	Donetsk People's Republic
DPSU	State Border Guard Service (Ukraine)
EU	European Union
EW	Electronic Warfare
FPV	first person view (drones)
FSB	Federal Security Service (Russian domestic security agency)
Gen.	General
GOU	Main Operations Directorate of the (Russian) General Staff
GRU	Main Intelligence Directorate (Russian military intelligence, technically renamed GU in 2010)
GU	Main Directorate of the General Staff (Russian military intelligence)
IFV	infantry fighting vehicle
Indep	Independent
LMV	Light Mobility Vehicle
LNR	Lugansk People's Republic
Lt.	Lieutenant
Maj.	Major
MANPADS	Man-Portable Air Defence System
Mech	Mechanized
MLRS	Multiple-Launch Rocket System
MRAU	Massed Missile-Aviation Strike
MVS	Ukrainian Ministry of Internal Affairs
NTsUO	National Defence Management Centre (Russian)
OMON	Mobile Special Designation Detachment (of Rosgvardiya)
Op	Operational
Plt	Platoon
Rgt	Regiment
Rosgvardiya	National Guard (Russia)
RPG	Rocket-Propelled Grenade [launcher]
SBU	Security Service of Ukraine
SOBR	Special Quick Response Detachment (of Rosgvardiya)
SOIMS	Service of Operational Information and International Relations of the FSB (5th Service)
SVO	Special Military Operation (Russian term for Ukraine war)
SVR	Foreign Intelligence Service (Russian)
UDO	State Protection Administration (Ukraine)
VDV	Air Assault Troops (Russian paratroopers)
VTO	Territorial Defence Forces (Ukraine)
ZSU	Ukrainian Armed Forces

CONTENTS

INTRODUCTION   4

ORIGINS   7
Warnings of war   8
Putin's echo chamber   11
The final decision   13

THE PLAN   15
How the war was not planned   16
The Hostomel bridgehead   20
Towards Kyiv   20
The wider invasion   23
The defence   23

THE OPERATION   26
Decapitation averted   27
The battle for Hostomel   29
The drive on Kyiv   44

ANALYSIS   68

CONCLUSION   76

FURTHER READING   79

INDEX   80

INTRODUCTION

We have been left no other option to protect Russia and our people, but for the one that we will be forced to use today. The situation requires us to take decisive and immediate action… I have decided to launch a special military operation.

Vladimir Putin, announcing the invasion, 24 February 2022

In many ways, Russia had been at war with Ukraine since 2014, when the 'Revolution of Dignity' toppled the corrupt but legitimately elected government of President Viktor Yanukovych. Protests against Yanukovych had been growing since autumn 2013, when the government reversed its position on signing an Association Agreement with the European Union (EU), openly admitting that it had come under pressure from Moscow, which had only belatedly realized that it would in effect lock Ukraine out of its own trading bloc, the Eurasian Economic Union. The protests grew and were largely mishandled by the government, which was heavy-handed when it needed to be conciliatory, uncertain when it needed to show confidence. A permanent protest in Kyiv's Maidan Square became violent and, as crowds clashed with security forces in February 2014, the government fell, and Yanukovych fled to Russia.

Putin, who had long held the belief that the West was engaged in a campaign of deliberate subversion to topple governments of which it did not approve, saw this as just another example of, as one member of a conservative Russian think tank close to the Kremlin put it, 'CIA and MI6 regime change conspiracy'. Besides, he regarded Ukraine as within Moscow's legitimate sphere of influence, and assumed that any tilt towards the West might start with EU trade deals but end with NATO membership, or at least Western military assets based on Ukrainian soil.

In the immediate chaos which followed the collapse of the Yanukovych government, Russia seized the strategically vital peninsula of Crimea in an almost bloodless special operation.[1] As Russians of every political

---

1   See RAID 59, *Putin Takes Crimea 2014. Grey-zone warfare opens the Russia-Ukraine conflict*

complexion cheered what they saw as the righteous return of Crimea – which had been Russian until 1954 – anti-government forces were rising in south-eastern Ukraine's Donbas region, where the country's Russian speakers were disproportionately present. Most did not want to secede from Ukraine, but were concerned that the new regime was dominated by Ukrainian-speaking leaders from the Catholic west of the country, and that they might face

Z, one of the recognition codes used to tell Russian from Ukrainian vehicles, has become something of a symbol for the Kremlin's attempts to inspire a crusading spirit amongst its people. Here, a large 'New Year's Z' has been pointedly installed in front of the US Embassy in Moscow. (Getty)

discrimination. Most were simply looking for guarantees, and perhaps greater autonomy within Ukraine, but there were radicals who wanted outright independence or annexation by Moscow, and to their side flocked a motley collection of Russian volunteers, thugs, mercenaries, and opportunists, keen to fan the flames of civil war.

Putin had had no designs on the Donbas originally, but true to form, at first, he neither opposed nor encouraged the rebels and their allies, but waited to see what would happen, allowing his more hawkish officials to funnel weapons and money into the conflict on their own initiative. As the new Ukrainian government began to establish itself, and regular and volunteer forces closed in on the self-proclaimed rebel 'people's republics' of Donetsk and Lugansk (DNR and LNR, respectively), though, he decided that they were too useful an instrument

THE BATTALION TACTICAL GROUP

Although the battalion tactical group has a long pedigree in Soviet service, it really came to the fore during Sergei Shoigu's tenure as Defence Minister (2012–24), in which the focus was increasingly not on mass war so much as smaller intervention operations. The BTG is a combined-arms manoeuvre unit generated from within a brigade – then the basic building block of the Russian army – which could be deployed for offensive operations. Although the composition of a BTG varies depending on the brigade which spawned it, it typically comprises 2–4 mechanized companies, a tank company, and additional artillery, air-defence, engineering, and logistical units. The 600-800 soldiers in a BTG would generally all be volunteer *kontraktniki* (not least as Russian law prohibits requiring conscripts to serve

abroad except in time of declared war) and draw on a disproportionate share of the parent brigade's support units. Many, for example, would have not one but two anti-tank companies, 2–3 artillery batteries, and 2 air-defence batteries. As a result, they may actually end up with half the brigade's personnel and assets. The BTG turned out to be an effective formation for operations when flexibility and firepower, rather than staying power, were needed, but a poor choice for the kind of brutal, attritional fighting that characterised the war in Ukraine. Put simply, it has too few infantry – usually only 200 or so – to be able to absorb losses and hold ground. Just as the army began to swing back to the larger division instead of the brigade, so too the BTG lost its primacy in Ukraine.

The undeclared war in the Donbas in many ways lit the fuse for the 2022 invasion. Here, a pro-Russian fighter from Chechnya stands near a damaged Ukrainian APC in Debaltseve in 2015, after their capture of this strategic transport hub. (Getty)

Putin was encouraged in his ambitions towards Ukraine by the emerging democracy's often-volatile politics. Here riot police keep nationalist protesters away from the Rada, the parliament building, in central Kyiv, during long-running protests in 2016. (© Mark Galeotti)

of pressure and destabilization to let fall. Battalion tactical groups (BTGs) of regular Russian troops surged into the Donbas whenever the government forces looked set to crush the rebels, and Moscow took increasingly open control. By autumn 2014, what had begun more as an insurrection amongst Ukrainians had become an undeclared war by Russia against Ukraine.

Over the next seven years, though, Putin would not take the final step of annexing these pseudo-states. The Minsk I (2014) and Minsk II (2015) accords, which neither side truly embraced or applied, would have seen the DNR and LNR (but not Crimea) reincorporated into Ukraine, but with a degree of autonomy that Kyiv feared would make them essentially Russian 'Trojan horses'. Putin's aim, after all, was not to keep these increasingly impoverished and criminalized regions – though he would eventually annex them in September 2022 – but instead cynically to use them to unsettle Ukraine and grant him a virtual veto in Kyiv. The successive governments of Oleksandr Turchynov (February–June 2014), Petro Poroshenko (2014–19), and Volodymyr Zelensky (2019–) would not fall into this trap, though, and, by 2021, Putin was growing impatient and felt the need to raise the stakes, starting a major build-up of forces on Russia's borders with Ukraine.

ORIGINS

The problem is that in territories adjacent to Russia, which I have to note is our historical land, a hostile 'anti-Russia' is taking shape. Fully controlled from the outside, it is doing everything to bring in NATO armed forces and obtain cutting-edge weapons.
    Vladimir Putin, televised address on the eve of the invasion

In spring 2021, Putin began massing forces along the Ukrainian border. Meanwhile, a small circle of senior Russian officials appear to have begun drawing up plans for an invasion. Crucially, this was more than anything else a political rather than strictly military venture, and wholly or substantially outside the usual structures of the Main Operations Directorate (GOU) of the General Staff. Defence Minister Sergei Shoigu was involved (even though he reportedly had quiet misgivings about the whole idea), but he was not a professional soldier. Chief of the General Staff Gen. Valery Gerasimov was both involved and an experienced soldier, but it appears that he simply went along with Putin's wishes rather than ever challenge them. Otherwise, the majority of those involved appear instead to have been intelligence officers, such as Col. Gen. Sergei Beseda, head of the 5th Service of the Federal Security Service (FSB), or political appointees and presidential cronies such as Yuri Kovalchuk, the chair of Bank Rossiya (known as 'Putin's banker'). Indeed, in July 2021, the 5th Service's 9th Department, which specifically targets Ukraine, was upgraded in status to a full directorate. According to Ukrainian intelligence, it was expanded from around 25 staff to over 200 as it prepared plans for the country's destabilization.

Vladimir Putin observes the main stage of the Vostok ('East') 2022 strategic command post exercise, flanked by his then Defence Minister Sergei Shoigu, left, and Chief of the General Staff and First Deputy Defence Minister General Valery Gerasimov. (Russian Presidential Administration, CC 4.0)

At this stage, this was still only a contingency plan, and many of the more junior figures involved in this secretive process appear to have assumed it would never be invoked, not least because, as will be discussed below, it was based on what seemed implausible assumptions and broke many of the fundamental precepts of Russian military doctrine.

Instead, the build-up of forces appeared primarily to be a political and economic weapon. By summer 2021, more than 80,000 troops were camped either in the occupied Donbas regions or along the border. Meanwhile, in July Putin produced a lengthy and historically dubious essay, 'On the Historical Unity of Russians and Ukrainians,' which asserted that Ukraine, or at least the eastern part of the country, was essentially Russian.

Warnings of war

With Putin claiming a right to part of the country, and in the shadow of Russian tanks, Ukraine's economy began to falter, and foreign leaders flocked to Moscow in the hope of trying to persuade him not to invade. To many, this was the point: Putin was using his military precisely to bring pressure to bear on Kyiv, in the hope of forcing Zelensky, who had come to office sounding conciliatory towards Russia, to make a deal. Ultimately, this failed, both because Putin was in effect trying to force Ukraine into becoming a vassal state, and also because many of the issues on the ground relating to minority rights and past grievances were simply too intractable. Ultimately, Putin believed that ever since the Revolution of Dignity – itself in his mind an example of Western 'hybrid war' – Ukraine was being turned not just into a satellite of NATO, but a weapon to use against Russia. The potential for NATO troops or systems to be based there, let alone, as Kyiv wanted, the country actually joining the alliance, were all described as 'red lines' by Moscow. According to Russian strategic culture, the best defence in the face of such challenges is often a good offence or, as the military theorist Col. Alexander Bartosh wrote in the authoritative defence journal *Voyennaya Mysl* (Military Thought), 'only an offensive, and not a defensive,

ON THE HISTORICAL UNITY OF RUSSIANS AND UKRAINIANS

In this lengthy text, Putin claimed that Russia and Ukraine were 'parts of essentially the same historical and spiritual space,' tragically divided both by mistakes on both sides and the deliberate machinations of foreign enemies trying 'to pit the parts of a single people against one another.' Citing the origins of Ukraine, Belarus and Russia in the medieval Ancient Rus, Putin claimed that Ukrainian nationalism – and, indeed, the very idea of a separate Ukrainian state – was the construct of Polish settlers and isolated intellectuals in the 19th century, and when Lenin decreed the creation of a Ukrainian Soviet Socialist Republic within the new USSR in 1922, and included in the Soviet constitution republics' rights to secede from the Union, he planted a 'most dangerous time bomb,' leading to the country's fragmentation in 1991. Rambling, self-indulgent, shamelessly distorting and cherry-picking the facts to suit his argument, this piece of historical revisionism, with its closing assertion that the 'true sovereignty of Ukraine is possible only in partnership with Russia,' probably genuinely reflects Putin's beliefs, and certainly represented a manifesto for intervention.

Russian strategy in the hybrid war imposed on it [by the West] will ensure the implementation of the policy announced by the President of the Russian Federation of establishing at his own discretion 'red lines'.'

Nonetheless, Kyiv believed that Moscow was bluffing and would not risk a full-scale war. However, British and US intelligence were increasingly convinced that Putin intended to invade, especially after he began sending yet more troops to the border from October. They would in due course release unprecedented amounts of intelligence data to try and convince not only their allies, but also Kyiv itself. The Europeans and Ukrainians remained generally sceptical, though. Indeed, Kyiv would only really believe that there would be an attack some 72 hours before it happened, when Russian communications lit up with radio messages and their intercepts picked up bemused and dismayed commanders asking each other if Moscow had gone mad (while some were enthusiastic).

In November 2021, CIA Director William Burns had gone to Moscow to warn the Kremlin that its plans were no secret and of the dire consequences if they went ahead. Putin did not take the threats seriously, pointing to the muted response to the 2008 invasion of Georgia and 2014 annexation of Crimea, and he and his tame media rubbished any suggestions of an invasion. Yet this stood in contrast with Putin's increasingly ambitious agenda. Implicitly, in return for holding off from any invasion, in December he put

A column of Russian BMP-2 IFVs in the Asipovichy Training Ground in Belarus. The regular and sizeable Zapad ('West') exercises held between Belarusian and Russian forces proved useful as a way of trying to intimidate Kyiv – and moving forces closer to Ukraine's borders. (Getty)

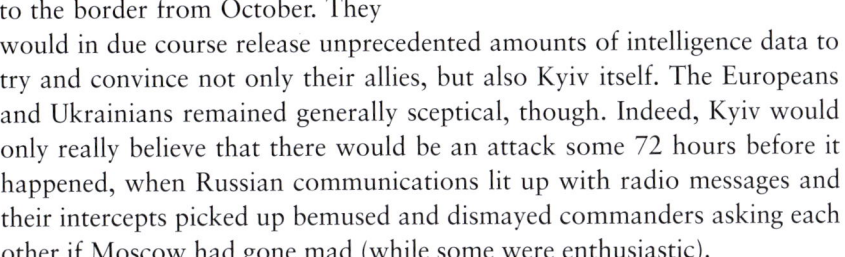

THE KIREYEV MYSTERY

Denys Kireyev was a Ukrainian banker with a fascination for the world of espionage and a wealth of contacts not only across the national political spectrum, but in Russia, too. This helps explain why, in 2021, he was recruited personally by Lt. Gen. Kyrylo Budanov, head of Ukrainian military intelligence (HUR), to use his connections to try and assess Russia's intentions. According to Budanov, on the eve of the invasion, Kireyev was able to tip him off not only that it was happening, but that the Antonov Airport would be a priority target. On 28 February, Kireyev was unexpectedly tapped to join a Ukrainian delegation which met in Belarus for (inconclusive) talks with their Russian counterparts

about a ceasefire. He was expected to take part in the second round of talks, too, but was picked up by a heavily armed team from the SBU. Less than two hours later, his body, shot in the head, was found lying in a street in central Kyiv. The SBU announced that they had killed a traitor, but HUR insisted that he was a patriot and a hero: after a funeral with full military honours, he was posthumously given the Order of Bohdan Khmelnytsky, III class. Nonetheless, while he is now remembered as a man who brought an eleventh-hour warning to Kyiv, whether he was a victim of a tragic misunderstanding (which is the official line) or a murderous turf war between the SBU and HUR, is still unclear.

For years, Ukraine had been working hard to recruit an army of well-motivated professionals. This poster, superimposing a modern soldier with images from the Cossack past, encourages passers-by to remember that 'there is such a profession: defender of the homeland.' (© Mark Galeotti)

forward a number of demands which extended beyond Ukraine to the whole security architecture of Europe. Not only did Putin want NATO to renounce any further eastward expansion – which would have affected not just Ukraine, but also prospective member Georgia – but in effect roll it back, with allied forces withdrawn from the former Warsaw Pact states of Central Europe, along with any intermediate-range missiles. Whether Putin really believed these terms might be accepted or whether he was simply creating a pretext for further military action, NATO rejected them and countered with a demand that Moscow withdraw its forces from the occupied territories of Ukraine and Georgia, as well as Moldova's ethnic Russian breakaway region of Transnistria. The Russian Ministry of Foreign Affairs stiffly responded that when 'red lines and core security interests' were ignored, Russia reserved the right to apply unspecified 'military-technical measures.'

Meanwhile, the large-scale Russian–Belarusian *Soyuznaya Reshimost* (Allied Resolve) military exercises, scheduled for 10–20 February, saw up to 30,000 troops assembled, including a sizeable contingent from the Eastern Military District: a perfect excuse to transfer yet more forces to the region, where there were now 136 BTGs drawn from Russia's eleven Combined Arms Armies and one Tank Army. In total this force amounted to 190,000 troops. More to the point, the 'tail' elements to complement the 'teeth', which would be required for any serious military intervention, were also beginning to be deployed, from fuel bowsers to pontoon bridges. The assembly of other logistical requirements, not least fresh blood packs for transfusions, also pointed to an imminent intervention. At the same time, tensions along the line of contact in the Donbas flared up, with monitors from the Organization for Security and Cooperation in Europe recording thousands of ceasefire violations, largely initiated by Russian and DNR/LNR forces. The Russian state-controlled media, however, reported these as provocations from the Ukrainian government side.

On 19 February, at the Munich Security Conference, President Zelensky incautiously challenged Kyiv's continued commitment to the 1994 Budapest Memorandum on Security Assurances, whereby Ukraine had renounced the remaining Soviet-era nuclear weapons still on its territory, whose launch codes were in any case in Russian hands. Despite the common assumption that the memorandum embodied some security guarantees, all the signatories (Russia, the USA, and the UK) really committed themselves to was not attacking Ukraine and bringing any breaches of this to the United Nations. Although Ukraine had neither the capacity nor intention of acquiring nuclear weapons, Zelensky's words were then exploited by Putin and Shoigu further to present Kyiv as a threat to Russia, eager to become a nuclear power. The pretexts and the forces were ready: all Putin needed now was to make a final decision.

Putin's echo chamber

It may sound implausible, but the truth is that as of perhaps ten days before the actual invasion, Putin may well still not have absolutely made up his mind whether to invade, and, if so, quite what the objective would be: a full-scale assault aimed at imposing a puppet government in Kyiv, or a more

limited operation simply to take the south and south-east of the country, securing all of the Donbas and the so-called 'land bridge' connecting Crimea to the Russian mainland. Despite the bare-chested machismo of his public image, he tends to be cautious, holding off making tough calls as long as he can. While Western leaders had been trying to warn him off any intervention – French President Emmanuel Macron and German Chancellor Olaf Scholz both went to Moscow for this very reason – these were not the people to whom Putin was willing to listen.

While in theory Foreign Minister Sergei Lavrov, left, was more important than erstwhile Secretary of the Russian Security Council Nikolai Patrushev, right, in practice the latter's closer connections with Putin meant that he was far more influential. This was especially the case after worsening relations with the West following the 2014 annexation of Crimea offered more scope for his hawkish conspiracy theories. (Getty)

Ultimately, he seems to have concluded that a full-scale invasion actually posed relatively little risk. No one in his circle of friends and cronies disagreed. They, after all, knew that their continued presence in that charmed circle – with all the opportunities for power and wealth it entailed – depended on keeping Putin happy, which essentially meant telling him what he wanted to hear, not what he needed to hear. Thus, he was only really listening to a mix of hawks, nationalists, and yes-men, none of whom were willing to dispel his fantasies of a quick and easy triumph.

Amongst the former were figures such as Nikolai Patrushev and Alexander Bortnikov. As long-serving secretary of the powerful Security Council, KGB veteran Patrushev was in effect the closest thing to a national security adviser in Putin's Kremlin, a man convinced that NATO sought to marginalize, if not dismantle, Russia, and that Ukraine was simply the latest battlefield in this undeclared political war. Bortnikov, his successor as head of the FSB, was less outspoken, but essentially shared the same views as his patron and predecessor Patrushev. He was also influenced by Col. Gen. Beseda's reassurances that the 5th Service had thoroughly penetrated the Ukrainian government and armed forces, and that hundreds of turncoats were ready to declare for Moscow's puppet government, something that turned out to be far from the case.

The nationalists included the aforementioned Kovalchuk, as well as the pro-Kremlin Ukrainian businessman and politician Viktor Medvedchuk, a personal friend of Putin's (who was godfather to one of his daughters). While Kovalchuk was more bullish about Russia and Ukraine being really

Especially controversial have been the claims that the Russian Orthodox Church has been used for Moscow's intelligence and influence operations, deepening a split within the Ukrainian Orthodox community. Here, SBU officers secure the grounds of the St. George Cathedral in Lviv. (Getty)

just one nation, Medvedchuk – who regarded them as separate nations, but 'with intertwined histories, religion' – was deeply hostile to the Zelensky government and was accused of funding Donbas separatists, such that his assets were frozen in 2021. He may have been considered by Putin as a suitable proxy leader to be imposed on Kyiv after the invasion, but either way seems to have been very supportive of an intervention. Central to this group's views was the pernicious line that Ukraine was in the hands of 'Nazis' somehow bent on a genocide of the Russian-speaking population.

Even more numerous, though, were the yes-men who, even while often having their doubts, simply went along with Putin's fantasies, afraid of losing their privileged positions. Defence Minister Shoigu, who had also reportedly been lukewarm about the annexation of Crimea, raised no objections. He was, in fairness, not a career soldier and may not have fully understood how the plan clashed with doctrinal guidance for how such a conflict – a 'regional war' in official Russian terms – ought to be waged. Gen. Gerasimov certainly did, though, and yet remained silent, even though a key part of his role was precisely to be the voice of the General Staff. Sergei Naryshkin, head of the Foreign Intelligence Service (SVR) was undoubtedly being briefed about the degree to which the Americans and the British had uncovered the evolving battle plans as well as the real mood in Ukraine, but he was no more able or willing to raise this with the president than Foreign Minister Sergei Lavrov. In general, there were many senior officials who had reason to doubt Putin's confidence, but who failed to stand up, maintaining the echo chamber around the president.

THE FSB AND UKRAINE

The FSB's 5th Service, the Service of Operational Information and International Relations (SOIMS), is ostensibly largely responsible for liaison relationships with other intelligence services, but its Department of Operative Information (DOI) has increasingly been involved in overseas operations, as the FSB moves into territory previously staked out by military intelligence and the Foreign Intelligence Service (SVR). Given that the SVR was previously bound by treaty not to spy on most post-Soviet states, this was a particular role for the FSB. The DOI's 9th Department focuses on Ukraine, and since 2014 had been especially active developing agent networks. In a sign of its growing role, in 2021 it was upgraded to a full directorate. Col. Gen. Beseda, head of the 5th Service, was closely involved with its work – he had even been in Kyiv during the 2014 Revolution of Dignity – and its massive and largely futile effort to use them to destabilize Ukraine in 2022.

The final decision

That Putin had given even his highest officials no clear steer as to his thinking became evident on 21 February 2022. On that day, the heads of the DNR and LNR, Denis Pushilin and Leonid Pasechnik respectively, appealed to Putin with a request to recognize them as fully independent states, and also formally to commit itself to their 'protection.' They would not, needless to say, have done this without being directed to do so by the Kremlin. In response, Putin held a largely televised meeting of his Security Council, an advisory body bringing together not just the heads of the military and security services, but also other key officials from the Presidential Administration and the cabinet. What ensued was a painful exercise in sycophancy, as otherwise powerful figures clearly tried to guess what the president wanted to hear, while Putin slapped them down when they were wrong.

A T-72 tank of the LNR's armed forces that, after annexation, would be incorporated into the Russian armed forces. (Getty)

Dmitry Kozak, deputy head of the Presidential Administration and Putin's key interlocutor with Kyiv, was shut down when he tried to argue against annexing the Donbas. Putin, who enjoys petty exercises of power, tormented an obviously nervous Naryshkin when he mumbled and fumbled his lines. On the other hand, Gen. Viktor Zolotov, a former bodyguard of Putin's and now head of the National Guard, was listened to respectfully when he claimed, with more loyalty than accuracy, that Russia does:

> not border on Ukraine, we have no border with Ukraine. This is the *Americans'* border, because they are the masters in that country, while the Ukrainians are their vassals. And the fact that they are rushing weapons to Ukraine and are trying to create nuclear arsenals [that] will come back to hurt us in the future.

Even Patrushev counselled accepting an American offer of talks, while Interior Minister Vladimir Kolokoltsev went the other way, unrealistically proposing not only that the DNR and LNR be recognised, but also with boundaries extending deep into territories still held by the Ukrainian government. Everyone made their guesses at to what would please the de facto tsar, and Putin gave no clues when he closed, thanking them for their opinions and promising a decision soon.

As a man obsessed with his legacy, he clearly decided that history awaited him. Later that day, he formally recognized the statehood of the DNR and LNR. The next day, he requested permission from the Federation Council, the upper chamber of the Russian legislature, to send in 'peacekeepers'. This was a technicality, and he duly received it. Already, on the 21st, sealed orders had been distributed to commanders along the frontier, generating

Gen. Viktor Zolotov, the commander of the Rosgvardiya, who fiercely supported the invasion that would leave so many of his own National Guardsmen dead or wounded – and many of the rest embittered at being thrown unprepared into a full-scale war. (Russian Presidential Administration, CC 4.0)

the shock and dismay Kyiv's interception stations had registered. The last preparations began to be made.

Early in the morning of 24 February, a pre-recorded speech from Putin announced a 'Special Military Operation' (SVO) intended to 'protect' the peoples of the DNR and LNR by 'demilitarizing and denazifying Ukraine.' He added that:

> It is not our plan to occupy Ukrainian territory. We do not intend to impose anything on anyone by force… The current events have nothing to do with a desire to infringe on the interests of Ukraine and the Ukrainian people. They are connected with defending Russia from those who have taken Ukraine hostage and are trying to use it against our country and our people.

Meanwhile, for all his claims about a limited and defensive goal, those 190,000 Russian troops were rolling into Ukraine from the north, the east, and the south, and the full-scale invasion had begun.

Ukrainian marines landing from Mi-8 helicopters during Exercise *Sea Breeze* 2019, a US and Ukrainian co-hosted multinational maritime exercise in the Black Sea. While an essential part of Kyiv's efforts to build closer relations with the West, such activities played into Putin's suspicions about its new allegiances. (Public Domain)

THE PLAN

Whoever tries to hinder us, or threaten our country or our people, should know that Russia's response will be immediate and will lead you to consequences that you have never faced in your history. We are ready for any turn of events. All necessary decisions in this regard have been made.

Vladimir Putin, announcing the invasion, February 24, 2022

When Russian forces headed to Kyiv, some were told to pack musical instruments, others dress uniforms, for the anticipated victory parade in a few days. Putin had apparently believed three days would be enough, at least to take the Ukrainian capital. In fairness, most of the same Western defence analysts who rightly anticipated war also assumed that Moscow would secure a quick victory, even if perhaps in weeks rather than days. It was not to be, though.

The crucial – and catastrophic – fundamental assumption behind the invasion plan was that Ukraine could quickly be decapitated of its political leadership and that the speed and decisive nature of Russia's advance, coupled with Western disarray, the activities of Moscow's agents and sympathizers, and widespread disillusion amongst the population (after all, Zelensky's approval ratings had been declining fast) would mean that there would be no organized or sustained resistance. Some units, such as the Azov Rgt (which was originally recruited largely from ultra-nationalists and neo-Nazis), would be expected to fight, but the belief that the main challenge would be street protests helps explain why a substantial proportion of the invading force was

The Russians were severely mistaken in their assumption that they would soon be able to stage a victory parade down Kyiv's main Kreshchatyk thoroughfare, the way they were used to in Moscow. (Russian Presidential Administration, CC 4.0)

By 2022, the Azov Regiment had formally dropped the 'wolfsangel' symbol also used by the Nazis, visible here on the gate of a base of theirs near Mariupol in 2019. That said, many of its soldiers still retained such symbols, despite official discouragement. (Getty)

While Putin was perfectly happy to visit the high-tech new National Defence Management Centre, he ultimately failed to use the capacities it was designed to provide in his invasion of Ukraine. (RPA, CC 4.0)

drawn from Rosgvardiya, Russia's National Guard, a paramilitary internal security force, rather than the regular army.

In short, Putin's use of the term 'Special Military Operation' was not simply a piece of propaganda, it also reflected his belief that this would not become a war. If anything, he seems to have believed that this would be closer to the special operation that seized Crimea, regardless of the massive differences between their scale and circumstances. Putin, it is worth remembering, had no meaningful military experience (a cursory term in reserve officer training while at university in the 1970s hardly counts) and was instead looking at the situation through the eyes of a former intelligence officer, not those of a soldier.

How the war was not planned

The irony is that the Russian General Staff has a very intellectual approach to warfighting, with everything from a clearly defined range of different scales of conflict through to algorithms to determine the optimal density of an artillery barrage. Accustomed to planning for the worst case, when planning for a full-scale invasion of a country with a population of over 44 million and more than 200,000 soldiers even before national mobilization – and eight years preparation for just such an attack – they would normally have followed a clear process. The GOU would take the lead in developing the plans, and it would set up what was known as a Combat Management Group within the recently established National Defence Management Centre (NTsUO). This would have brought together relevant specialists, from tacticians to logisticians, to address the parameters of the operation properly and establish exactly what resources would be needed. This would form the basis for any actual operational planning, a process that ideally would take months.

Yet the plans for the 2022 invasion were drawn up by a small group of officials working outside the usual chain of command, with discrete elements farmed out to others, often from the security apparatus rather than the GOU. They, in turn, were not made aware of how they fit into the whole project and, indeed, that they were working on an invasion plan, being told they were contingencies for 'demonstrative operations' or 'security precautions.' As it was, the NTsUO was apparently only activated on 21 February, the day Putin seemingly made his final decision. This would be painfully evident once the war started, with many units only having enough fuel, ammunition, and other consumables for a few days, or at the very most two weeks of operation – and the officers and men frequently taken by surprise that what they had been told were simply deployments on exercises had become a full-scale shooting war. Many were only told that they were invading Ukraine a few hours before moving.

According to the standard process for a major operation, there would be a degree of mobilization to bring combat units up to full strengths. As it was, many also went into battle still at peacetime strengths, so it would not be unusual to see tanks deployed without infantry cover (which is often suicidal) or APCs sent into action crewed, but with no personnel to carry. A single operational command structure would be established, but in this case at the start of this war there were up to five separate commanders in charge of different fronts, who ended up competing for resources and reinforcements. Finally, the war would open with a devastating preliminary Massed Missile-Aviation Strike (MRAU) designed to disrupt enemy air defences, smash their air force on the ground, blast bridges, cut supply lines, and hammer any concentrations of forces. Instead, the MRAU was a distinctly half-hearted and poorly planned venture, perhaps with the assumption that it made little sense destroying assets that would soon be in Russian control. This would mean that Kyiv would still be able to contest its skies as well as the ground. As a retired Russian officer who had served in the NTsUO later complained to me, 'I would have been hard-pressed to come up with a worse plan, even as a junior lieutenant.' So what was the actual plan?

Decapitation

The first element of the plan for the SVO was to prevent any effort at a coordinated defence by disrupting communications and the chain of command through electronic warfare (EW), cyberattacks, and the activities of agents within the Ukrainian chain of command who would fail to pass on messages, spread disinformation, or simply desert their posts. There was an ambitious programme for their activities, which would also include marking out landing zones for aerial assaults, securing or sabotaging infrastructure, and misdirecting the Ukrainians. The reality proved much less impressive. There were some successes, to be sure. Russia's capacity to take (if not hold) the southern city of Kherson was very much helped by the way that local security chief Gen. Serhii Kryvoruchko had evacuated

The Krasukha-2 is part of a suite of Russian electronic warfare assets which have given Moscow a distinct edge when used correctly. The Krasukha-2 is designed to jam GPS signals and the radars of airborne missiles and aircraft at ranges of up to 250km, while the more powerful Krasukha-4 can even affect satellites in Low Earth Orbit. (Vitaly Kuzmin, CC 3.0)

President Volodymyr Zelensky emerged as a powerful unifying symbol of an embattled Ukraine and advocate abroad. Here, flanked by an armed guard, he speaks at a press conference at his official residence the Maryinsky Palace shortly after the invasion. (Getty)

his personnel, in contravention of Zelensky's orders, while his deputy, Col. Ihor Sadokhin, reportedly passed them the locations of defensive minefields. However, many supposed agents proved unwilling or unable to carry out their missions, not least as the SBU and the rest of the Ukrainian security and law enforcement apparatus proved unexpectedly well able to counter and catch them.

Even more sinister was the decision to send small teams of GU (military intelligence) officers, including mercenaries and special forces operators, into Kyiv to capture or more likely kill President Zelensky and other key government figures. Part of the calculation was that without Zelensky, a highly effective communicator, the Ukrainians would find it harder to mobilize international support. Their orders were not to strike until an advance force of *Spetsnaz* commandos had reached the city limits and could secure a corridor for the assassins' escape, and in any case to wait for a final 'go' from Moscow.

Meanwhile, a death squad of Chechen gunmen drawn from the so-called Kadyrovtsy ('Kadyrovites') personally loyal to Ramzan Kadyrov, dictator of the Russian Chechen Republic, were also infiltrated into Kyiv in a parallel operation that seems largely connected to the FSB. They were to operate

THE HUNT FOR ZELENSKY

Kyiv, February 25, 2022. The details of the assassination attempts against President Zelensky and other senior officials – and the operations which foiled them – remain largely secret, but one incident reportedly involved a sniper from the Redut mercenary force, a former operator from the paratroopers' 45th Independent Guards *Spetsnaz* Brigade, armed with a heavy OSV-96 12.7mm anti-materiel rifle, with armour piercing rounds likely able to penetrate the roof or sides even of the president's armoured Mercedes-Benz S-Class. He was set up well away from the apartment window, to avoid being seen from outside. Either the team were under observation or, more likely, there was a tip-off, because the sniper's nest in a building overlooking one entry into Bankova Street, site of the Presidential Administration offices, was raided before any assassination attempt could be made. Commandoes from UDO, the State Protection Administration, armed with a Czech-made Skorpion Evo 3 submachine gun and an AKS-74 assault rifle burst in on the sniper and his spotter, who is wearing Ukrainian police uniform and armed with an AKS-74U assault carbine.

The Kamov-52 Alligator is not only a highly capable attack helicopter, in the Ukraine war it has also increasingly been used as a drone hunter-killer, with its side-mounted Shipunov 2A42 30mm autocannon and Igla-V air-to-air missiles. (KAMOV KA-52, CC 4.0)

entirely separately from the Russians being run by the GU – who were not even told of their existence – as a potential fallback.

The Hostomel bridgehead

The second main component of the initial plan was for some 300 paratroopers from the 11th Indep Guards Air Assault Bde and *Spetsnaz* operators from the 45th Guards *Spetsnaz* Bde in 24 Mi-8AMTSh helicopters, escorted by 10 Ka-52 and Mi-24/35M gunships, to launch a raid to seize Antonov (or Hostomel) Airport at the township of Hostomel, 10km northwest of Kyiv. The mission was commanded by the 45th Bde's Col. Vadim Pankov, an experienced combat veteran who had fought in the Chechen wars, the seizure of Crimea, and the subsequent Donbas conflict.

Unlike Kyiv Boryspil International Airport and Igor Sikorsky Kyiv International Airport (Zhuliany), Antonov was a cargo airport, with a 3.5km long runway suitable for the largest of Russian military transports. This made it an ideal choice for an airbridge. After all, it was also the base of the sole Antonov An-225 Mriya, the heaviest cargo aircraft ever built. The plan was therefore that once the airport was under Russian control, more troops and armoured forces could be landed quickly to invest Kyiv itself. To this end, at least two BTGs from the 76th Guards Air Assault Div were prepared for embarkation onto Il-76MD transport aircraft at their base in Pskov for quick deployment to Hostomel.

Towards Kyiv

Although the hope had apparently been that the Hostomel gambit would allow rapid entry into Kyiv, there was an awareness that the forces which could be airlifted in would be too few and too light to guarantee taking the capital, and that the operation, in any case, was not the same as securing

VOLODYMYR ZELENSKY

Volodymyr Zelensky was an unlikely war leader. A former comedian who had performed in both Russia and Ukraine, he was in many ways catapulted to power by the way his character in the TV series *Servant of the People* – a teacher unexpectedly elected president on the back of a viral video of his tirade against corruption and incompetence in government – resonated with the public. His electoral platform in 2019 included a pledge to try and mend relations between Russians and Ukrainians but, rebuffed and belittled by Moscow, he was already hardening his line before the invasion, even as his poll ratings dropped. The invasion, though, brought his capacity to connect with ordinary Ukrainians to the fore and he proved an inspirational national icon. Leaving much day-to-day administration to his chief of staff, his old friend Andrii Yermak, he focused his talents on encouraging and where necessary brow-beating the outside world into supporting Ukraine's struggle.

the country. Besides, a city with almost three million inhabitants would require extensive forces to control and pacify it. In a pincer movement, two armoured columns would converge on Kyiv from east and west.

Some 50,000 troops largely from the Eastern Military District (the 5th, 29th, 35th and 36th Combined Arms Armies) would strike south from allied Belarus. Under Col. Gen. Alexander Chaiko, commander of the Eastern Military District, they would pass through the still radioactive Chernobyl Exclusion Zone, then head down the western bank of the Dnipro River via Ivankiv and Demydiv. To distinguish themselves from the Ukrainians, who largely used the same vehicles and equipment, they bore the tactical marking V (from *Vostochny*, 'Eastern').

Meanwhile, 30,000 men from the Central Military District's 2nd Guards and 41st Combined Arms Armies under Col. Gen. Alexander Lapin would push out from Russia's Bryansk region and Gomel in Belarus, through Chernihiv, and head down along the river's eastern bank to take Kyiv from the northeast, via the town of Brovary. They bore the tactical sign O. (The now-infamous Z, from *Zapadny*, Northern, was used, ironically enough, in the southern offensive, although over time, as units were moved and redeployed, these codes became increasingly interchangeable.)

The expectation was that, thanks to the chaos created by the decapitating strikes and the airborne assault via Antonov Airport, these forces would have taken Kyiv by 27 February, where they could be refuelled and resupplied, so that most could continue further into Ukraine while a mix of regular troops and Rosgvardiya closed Moscow's grip on the capital. Ironically, more attention seems to have been given the post-conquest pacification

The rising sun casts its first rays on Kyiv, including the towering Motherland Monument, originally built to celebrate victory in the Second World War, but since the invasion repurposed as an icon of national resistance, with the hammer and sickle on the shield replaced by the tryzub, the three-pronged trident that is Ukraine's national symbol. (Getty)

AN-225 MRIYA

A one-of-a-kind, record-breaking heavy-lift aircraft, the Antonov An-225 was originally developed during the 1980s to transport the USSR's Buran space shuttle. Based on the already-huge An-124, the An-225 had a wingspan of fully 88m and was kept aloft by six Progress D-18T turbofan engines, two more than the An-124. It flew its maiden flight in 1988, but with the collapse of the Soviet space programme – and then the Soviet Union – it was mothballed in 1991, until Antonov Airlines refurbished it and brought the plane back into operational use in 2002. It acquired a niche role lifting oversized payloads, such as wind turbines from China to Denmark and locomotives from Germany to China. It was essentially destroyed during the battle for Hostomel, but a second, unfinished version which had languished in a two-thirds state of completion for years is due to be finished, in part using components salvaged from the first. In what some consider an act of official vindictiveness, in 2023 prosecutors charged the former head of Antonov, Serhii Bychkov, with 'negligence' for not having ordered the An-225 evacuated ahead of the invasion.

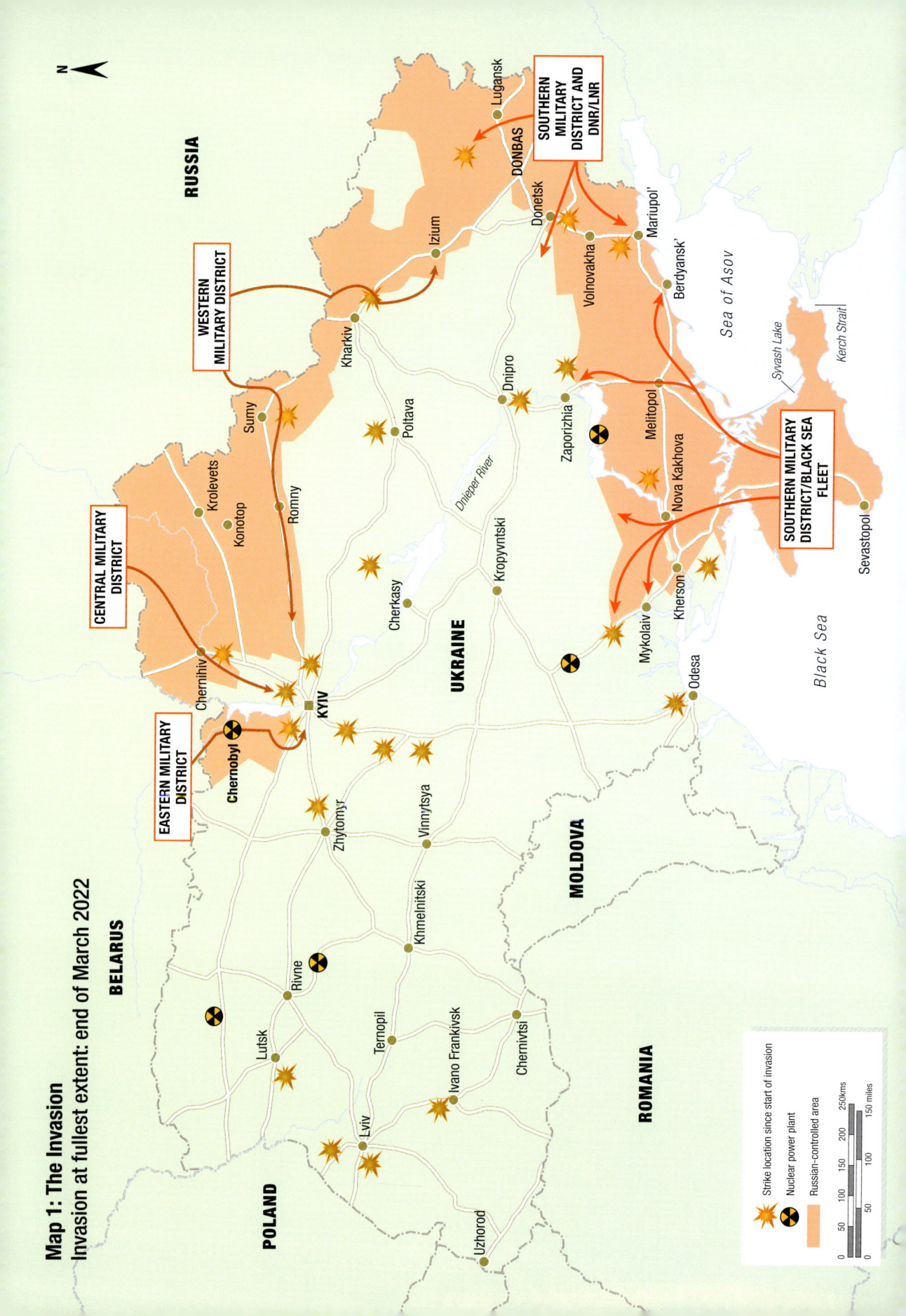

Map 1: The Invasion
Invasion at fullest extent: end of March 2022

N

RUSSIA

BELARUS

POLAND

MOLDOVA

ROMANIA

UKRAINE

DONBAS

Lugansk

Izium

Donetsk

Volnovakha

Mariupol'

Berdyansk'

Sea of Asov

Sevash Lake

Kerch Strait

Kharkiv

Dnipro

Zaporizhia

Melitopol

Nova Kakhova

Kherson

Mykolaiv

Odesa

Black Sea

Sevastopol

Sumy

Krolevets

Konotop

Romny

Poltava

Dniepper River

Cherkasy

Kropyvnitski

Chernihiv

KYIV

Chernobyl

Zhytomyr

Vinnytsya

Khmelnitski

Rivne

Lutsk

Ternopil

Ivano Frankivsk

Chernivtsi

Lviv

Uzhorod

WESTERN MILITARY DISTRICT

CENTRAL MILITARY DISTRICT

EASTERN MILITARY DISTRICT

SOUTHERN MILITARY DISTRICT AND DNR/LNR

SOUTHERN MILITARY DISTRICT/BLACK SEA FLEET

Strike location since start of invasion

Nuclear power plant

Russian-controlled area

0   50   100   150   200   250kms

0   50   100   150 miles

campaign than the actual invasion, with detailed guidance on how the city was to be divided into sectors that could be cordoned off, so that Rosgvardiya forces could conduct 'filtration' operations, identifying and detaining members of the security forces or others whom Moscow thought potentially dangerous.

The wider invasion

Meanwhile, although largely beyond the scope of this book, Russian troops were

advancing on a series of other fronts, each marked by their own recognition symbol. In the north, there was also a push towards Sumy, which bogged down in urban combat in the city itself. From the occupied Donbas, regular and DNR/LNR troops spilled out towards Kharkiv to the north and Mariupol to the south (of which only the latter was captured). To the south, forces from Crimea quickly advanced towards the city of Kherson, which they took and briefly held, then on to Mykolaiv, while other forces pushed northeast to join the attack on Mariupol to secure the 'land bridge' along the northern coast of the Sea of Azov.

However, the expectation was that the crucial thrust would be at Kyiv. Once the Ukrainian leadership had been killed, forced to flee, or imprisoned then a 'loyal' transitional government would be stood up, backed by Russian might. According to the Ukrainian constitution, in the absence of the president the Speaker of the Verkhovna Rada, the parliament, becomes acting leader. Putin's friend Medvedchuk, who had been a parliamentarian and led the pro-Moscow Ukrainian Choice movement, could have been imposed as Speaker and thus acting president – indeed, Zelensky later said Putin demanded he step down in Medvedchuk's favour. Then, the invading forces would have been officially welcomed as 'peacekeepers.'

The defence

However, ever since 2014 the Ukrainians had been planning, training, and arming for what many regarded as an inevitable war with Putin's Russia. Although the political leadership, convinced it understood the Kremlin better than the Americans or the British, was slow and reluctant to realize that this day was coming soon, many within the military were much more willing to accept the intelligence they were being presented. More to the point, the contingency planning for a Russian assault had never stopped. Defence spending, which had dropped to under 1% of GDP (according to Ukrainian figures) had been brought up to 2.7% by 2020, such that the Ukrainian

General Alexander Lapin, left, at an award ceremony in 2022. Note the Makarov pistol tucked into his chest pouch, and the blood group ribbon on his right shoulder: even generals in the combat zone know they are potentially at risk. (Mil. ru, CC 4.0)

Mariupol had been a particular target for the Russians and their Donbas proxies, given its strategic position on the Azov Sea coast ever since 2014, when these Ukrainian troops with their BMP-2 IFV were guarding against a separatist attack. (Getty).

armed forces (ZSU) had been grown from 165,000 in 2014 to 200,000 by 2022. The maverick militias which had emerged in 2014 were brought under tighter central control, largely in the National Guard and the Territorial Defence Forces (VTO), and a new Special Operations Forces Command was established.[2] These separate forces would often be the sources of some of the most innovative ideas adopted by the Ukrainians, such as the use of commercial First Person View (FPV) drones, initially for reconnaissance but in due course jerry-rigged with explosives for an attack role.

The Ukrainians were, however, mistaken on the likely scale and direction of any attack. In December 2021, Defence Minister Oleksii Reznikov had admitted the danger of a 'large-scale escalation' by Russia at the end of the coming January. However, the assumption was that this would primarily be directed at extending Russian control to the rest of the Donbas, and forces were thus concentrated along the eastern line of contact. Indeed, when the US government asserted at the end of 2021 that Russia could deploy over 175,000 troops in an invasion, Reznikov replied that as Ukraine had a regular army of 250,000 and could call on another 650,000 veterans and reservists, '175,000 [is] not enough.'

Even so, over the previous eight years, a nationwide defence programme had been developed that included not just the Territorial Defence Forces but also placing caches of weapons and explosives to support behind-the-lines partisan operations, the training of citizens in basic guerrilla skills, and the creation of fallback communications networks that also mobilized the ingenuity and enthusiasm of volunteers. Hackers would prove crucial in resisting Russian cyberattacks, for example, and a constant flow of reports about troop movements from ordinary civilians, posted on social media, provided a real-time picture of the invaders' strengths and locations. As tensions increased, the intelligence and security services stepped up their activities identifying and arresting presumed enemy agents, and Kyiv began reopening and renovating its 4,500 bomb shelters. More specifically, engineers from the 72nd Mech Bde, which was the main unit tasked with defending the capital, working

2   See ELI 228 *Armies of Russia's War in Ukraine*

TERRITORIAL DEFENCE FORCES

The Territorial Defence Forces (VTO) are reserve and auxiliary formations of the ZSU, the armed forces, which emerged to bring together most of the Territorial Defence Battalions, various volunteer militia units which emerged during the undeclared war with Russian-backed insurgents in the Donbas from 2015. In 2022, they were formally integrated into the ZSU, and, by March, some 100,000 new and existing VTO volunteers had been mustered, with a core of experienced veterans providing training and command. The VTO are organized into regional Territorial Defence Bdes of 5–9 bns, in theory each with an establishment strength of 492 but in practice unit strengths do vary considerably. VTO troops are essentially motorized infantry, although some brigades do have an attached company of tanks, and equipment is usually relatively basic, with some still using older 7.62mm AKM-47 rifles instead of the 5.45mm AK-74s that were the standard weapon of both the Russian and Ukrainian armies.

on the assumption that if there was an attack on the city it would come from the north-northeast via Chernihiv, surveyed that stretch of the border to identify likely invasion routes. From this, they decided that the E95 highway, from Gomel in Belarus to Chernihiv and then on to Kyiv, was the best, if not only viable, one for armoured forces. Plans were beginning to be made to destroy the bridge in Novi Yarylovychi, 6km south of the border, to delay any advance – although the Russians did have bridging equipment – but they were not sufficiently advanced by the time of the actual attack.

Although thousands of guns were distributed to volunteers, there were never enough, and here a new recruit to Kyiv's 112th Territorial Defence Brigade hefts his wooden training rifle in preparation for a Russian assault on the city that never came. (Getty)

Ukraine's friends also began taking action. The USA stepped up its supplies of ordnance, especially FGM-148 Javelin antitank missiles (some 150 launchers with more than 1,000 missiles) and, later, FIM-92 Stinger MANPADS. The British likewise delivered 2,000 shorter-range NLAW (Next-generation Light Anti-tank Weapon) missiles, while the RAF stepped up flights of its RC-135W Rivet Joint surveillance aircraft over the Black Sea to monitor Russian movements and communications, supplementing American E-8C Joint Surveillance Target Attack Radar System (JSTARS), RC-135W, and RQ-4 Global Hawk drone sorties. Nonetheless, with the Americans also gloomily anticipating that the Russians would win easily and quickly there were also those counselling caution. As one Pentagon official quietly admitted at an event in late January, 'my concern is that we will simply be handing weapons and equipment to the Russians for them to examine, use or sell.'

With its capacity to fire in either direct or top-strike modes, as well as its relatively advanced optics, the Javelin was crucial to blunting the Russian advance from the beginning. (Getty)

THE OPERATION

The fight is here; I need ammunition, not a ride.

Volodymyr Zelensky, on being offered evacuation by the USA, February 2022

Early on 24 February, at around 0340, the first Russian forces began crossing the line of contact in the Luhansk region. Some twenty minutes later, the news reached Lt. Gen. Serhii Deineko, head of the State Border Guard Service (DPSU), and he immediately passed the word on to Interior Minister Denys Monastyrsky. At 0420 he, in turn, woke President Zelensky with the stark message: 'it's begun.' As more and more reports of border crossings, including footage from emplaced cameras, began flooding into the DPSU headquarters, at 0517 Deineko sent the president a text:

During the operations to kill or capture – usually kill – Russian saboteurs and assassins in Kyiv, an SBU operator with yellow recognition armband covers the building opposite with his M4-WAC-47. This domestically produced rifle based on the AR-15 was intended to replace the AK-74. (Getty)

Good morning, dear Mr President. Allow me to report. This is a full-scale military aggression on the part of the Russian Federation. Several checkpoints on the border with Russia have been shelled; rockets from Grads are being fired from their territory. Jet aircraft can be heard flying over the Chornobyl area. Grad rockets are also being fired from Crimea. There are five casualties so far. My units are taking their positions.

Just over ten minutes later, Putin formally announced the SVO, as 150 cruise and ballistic missiles began their flights towards Ukraine's cities and installations. The defenders' communications and radar began to experience jamming, and a wave of Eniks E95M drones, typically used as targets, crossed into Ukrainian airspace, simulating attacking aircraft. When AD systems went active to shoot them down, they revealed themselves to the Russians, who engaged them with missiles. The initial invasion, needless to say, failed to go to plan, hamstrung as it was by the unrealistic assumptions on which it was based. That said, as will be explored later, things could have gone differently had the Russians been luckier or more willing to incur casualties.

Decapitation averted

The details of the Russian assassination operation in Kyiv remain, understandably, murky. The suggestion is that up to 400 mercenaries from the Wagner Group – essentially a public-private partnership used as a deniable Kremlin front – had already been covertly deployed in Kyiv, where for weeks they had been tracking their targets, from President Zelensky and Prime Minister Denys Shmyhal downwards. In some cases, this entailed physical surveillance, but they also used scanners to follow the movements of the mobile phones of their targets and their aides. However, there is also evidence that Wagner was deliberately excluded from the invasion, not least because the GU by then had its own pet mercenary army, Redut. The likelihood is that the would-be assassins, who probably numbered far fewer than 400 given that only around 60 were reported as killed or captured, were individually hired from Wagner and other mercenary forces, including Redut, or else were regular *Spetsnaz* commandos. However, it was presumably because these operatives stood a good chance of being killed or captured that GU did not use its own Unit 29155, the hit squad implicated in such actions as planting explosives in ammunition stocks intended for Ukraine in a warehouse in the Czech Republic in 2014 and the attempted assassination of defector Sergei Skripal in 2018.

In any case, the main Russian forces never managed to open up the promised escape corridor, and Moscow temporized, holding off unleashing the assassins while there was the potential for negotiation. Understandably, the Russian operators were increasingly concerned, not least as the longer

REDUT

Although the Wagner Group is best known in the West, the apparent success of the model of an ostensibly private army that could also be used as a deniable instrument of the Kremlin spawned rivals and successors. Many were much more tightly under the control of the defence ministry and the GU, especially Redut (Redoubt). Its genesis was in a private security firm set up in 2003 by veterans from the 45th Indep Guards Airborne Assault Bde, the paratroopers' own *Spetsnaz* unit. Over time, it grew, even while retaining its links to the ministry, and as Russian companies in Syria began offering contracts for heavily armed convoy and plant security, it became increasingly militarized. By 2018, Redut, sometimes going under the name *Shchit* (Shield), was increasingly obviously the ministry's favoured mercenary force, as relations with Wagner and its mercurial owner Yevgeny Prigozhin worsened. GU deputy head Lt Gen. Vladimir Alexeyev increasingly promoted Redut over Wagner, and at the start of the invasion of Ukraine, deliberately froze the latter out of the operation. He felt that Redut was more capable and reliable and that he did not need Wagner anymore. As it was, Redut would suffer such heavy casualties in the first weeks of the war that it was no longer operational, and – much to Prigozhin's satisfaction – Alexeyev would have to turn back to Wagner.

Various special police rapid response and counter-terrorism teams were pressed into service to fight the invaders, such as this Tactical-Operational Response Team, which became the Khyzhak Brigade. Khyzhak means 'predator,' hence the patches modelled on the alien hunter from the science fiction film franchise. Note the Fort-221, locally produced versions of the Israeli Tavor CTAR21 5.56mm bullpup. (Getty)

they were at large in an increasingly militarized Kyiv, the greater the chance of their being caught. Eventually, the order was given to launch the attacks on the 25th, but arguably by then it was too late. The potential window of opportunity at the chaotic very start of the war was closed, and Zelensky's bodyguards from the State Protection Administration (UDO) and Security Service of Ukraine (SBU) had been substantially expanded. Nonetheless, at least two efforts were made to assassinate the president, both of which saw the attackers ambushed and killed. One involved Russians in Ukrainian uniforms who had seized two army vehicles, including a Strela-10 (SA-13) AA carrier, in the northern Obolon suburb to try and make it past security checkpoints into central Kyiv around noon on the 25th. The other, whose details are still unclear, seems to have been foiled by the UDO as the operators tried to set up a sniper position close to Bankova Street, site of the Presidential Administration offices.

Meanwhile, after Zelensky was filmed in a demonstrative walkabout along Kyiv's Khreschatyk Boulevard on Saturday 26 February, the Chechens began to make their move. From their safe house in the outskirts of the city, they sallied forth and hijacked an ambulance, believing it would allow them to make their way into the central government district known as the 'Triangle' despite the curfew. They had apparently been under surveillance, though. Indeed, the secretary of Ukraine's National Security and Defence Council, Oleksii Danilov, even claimed that this was thanks to a tip-off from inside the Russian FSB, from officers 'who do not want to take part in this bloody war,' although this could easily have been a piece of wilful disinformation intended to foster paranoia and division amongst the enemy. In any case, a few hours later the Chechens were stopped at a roadblock and were all killed or detained in the ensuing firefight. A second group of Chechens, who had only just left the safe house, were also ambushed by elements of the SBU's Alpha anti-terrorist commando force.

Zelensky and the rest of the leadership was safe and, instead, the population of Kyiv was alerted and armed. As volunteers assembled Molotov cocktails and threw up makeshift barricades against a Russian assault that never actually made it into the city, some 18,000 AK-47 rifles were issued to anyone who wanted one, on the first day alone. While the United States had offered to evacuate and shelter Zelensky, he remained in Kyiv, both to coordinate the response to the invasion and as a symbol of Ukrainian defiance.

The battle for Hostomel

The fight to take Hostomel started no more auspiciously for the Russians. At just before 0700, two 3M14 Kalibr cruise missiles were launched at the airport. One was aimed at the barracks cantonment of the airport's defence force, two companies from the National Guard's 4th Op Bde named after Serhii Mykhalchuk, but only hit the parade ground. The other hit close to a nearby housing block, but caused no casualties. Otherwise, nothing was done to suppress any defences, whether out of poor planning or to avoid signalling the Russians' plans. Meanwhile, the attack force had lifted off from VD Bolshoi Bokov Airport in Belarus, some 170 km to the north, and was flying at low altitude along the east bank of the Dnipro River, gunships to the fore. It was escorted by Su-27 and Su-35S fighters, although the disparity between the cruising speed of the interceptors and helicopters meant the former had to fly in loops to remain close, coordinated by an Il-20M airborne command post and, still over Belarusian airspace, a Beriev A-50 early warning and control aircraft. Despite a combination of heavy jamming and air attacks on radar sites along the Dnipro there was no way this force – especially as it was flying in daylight – could pass wholly undetected, not least as local residents started posting images on social media. Five MiG-29 interceptors from Ukraine's 40th Tactical Aviation Bde at Vasylkiv were scrambled and fired R-27 air-to-air missiles at the helicopters (possibly downing a Mi-24), but were swept aside by the Russian fighters: two MiG-29s were shot down. However, at around 1030, as they turned near the dam of the Kyiv Hydroelectric Plant to cross the wide expanse of the Kyiv Reservoir in their approach to Hostomel, they were hit by MANPADS from the ground: despite the use of flares to try and decoy the missiles from their targets, a gunship was shot down and a Mi-8 badly damaged, but still able to limp to the target.

The attacking force reached Hostomel at around 1100. At this point, the formation split: the gunships broke to the north, to engage the defences around the runway with their guns, rockets, and missiles, while the paratroopers' Mi-8s swung around towards the south, to land in fields just outside the airport perimeter from whence they could assault the barracks and control tower. Low cloud provided the attackers cover until their final approach. Reportedly, Maj. Vitalii Rudenko, in charge of the airport's defences, did not even know the attack force was near until he heard the helicopters through the murk.

He had done what he could to prepare. Trucks and fuel bowsers were parked along the runway to prevent any landings by fixed-wing aircraft, and he had deployed 20 of

The Sukhoi Su-35 'Super Flanker' is a highly improved version of the Su-27 air-defence fighter, a multirole aircraft that played a significant role in the early stages of the invasion, as both an air superiority interceptor and also a fast bomber. As well as mounting an internal 30mm Gryazev-Shipunov GSh-30-1 autocannon, it has 12 hardpoints (two wingtip rails and ten wing and fuselage stations) able to carry a mix of bombs, missiles, and reconnaissance pods. (Anna Zvereva, CC 2.0)

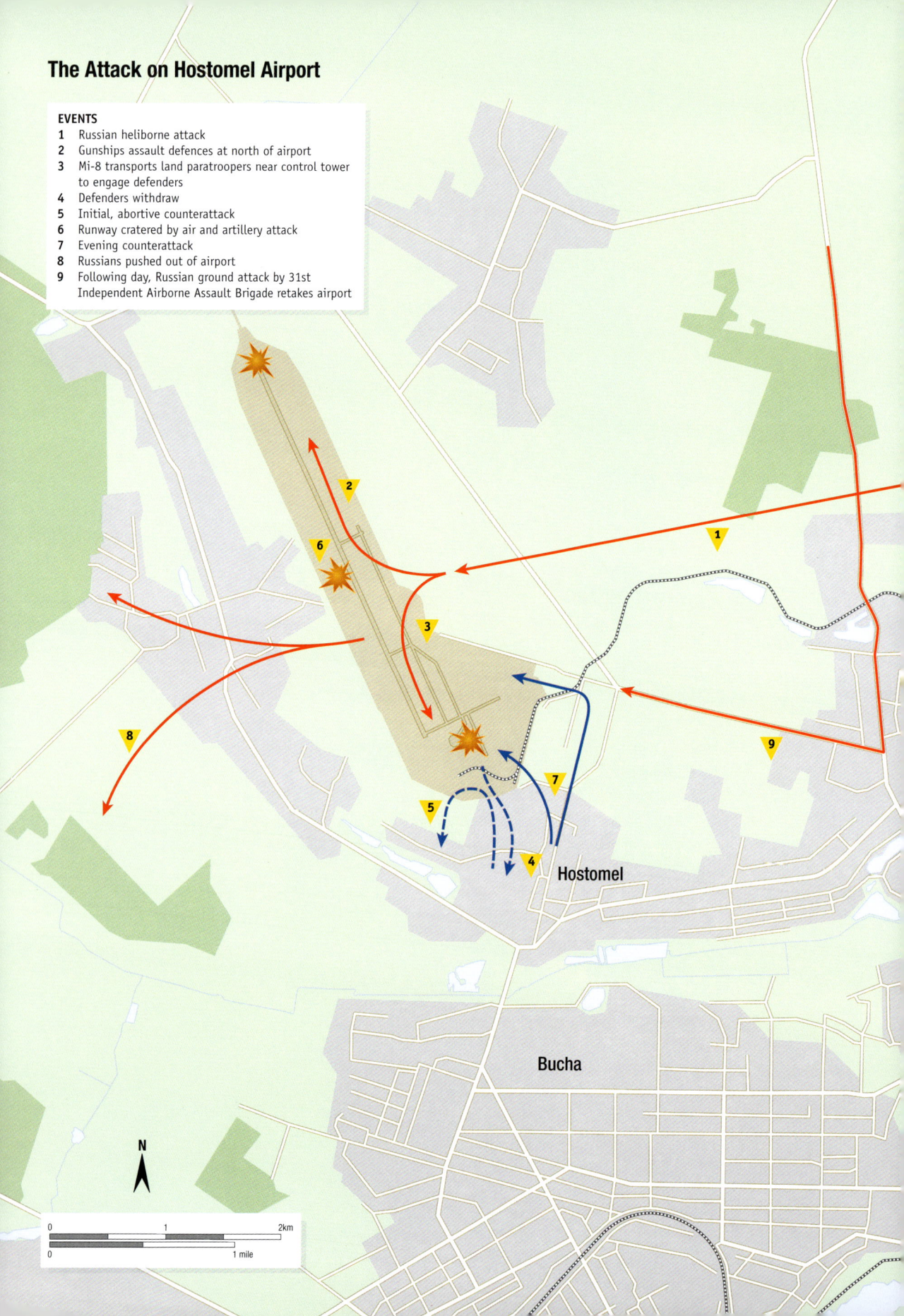

The Attack on Hostomel Airport

EVENTS

1 Russian heliborne attack
2 Gunships assault defences at north of airport
3 Mi-8 transports land paratroopers near control tower
   to engage defenders
4 Defenders withdraw
5 Initial, abortive counterattack
6 Runway cratered by air and artillery attack
7 Evening counterattack
8 Russians pushed out of airport
9 Following day, Russian ground attack by 31st
   Independent Airborne Assault Brigade retakes airport

Hostomel

Bucha

N

0   1   2km

0   1 mile

The ZU-23-2 is a distinctly dated system in use and production since the 1960s, but its simplicity, rugged build, and new role as an anti-drone weapon has seen it widely used during the Ukraine war. The twin 23mm autocannon have an effective range of 2.5km. (Getty)

his men to the north of the airport to defend its radar, entrusting them with his unit's dated ZU-23-2 23mm AA gun. The remainder of his force took up positions on the south side of the airport, where hangars, barracks, and administration buildings provided better cover. However, the gunships were able to suppress most of the improvised air defences relatively quickly. The ZU-23-2 gun was unable to score decisive hits and only one MANPADS team was able to draw blood, downing a Ka-52 with a 9K38 Igla (SA-18). The paratroopers were able to land in two waves and even though CIA Director William Burns had warned Kyiv during a secret visit in January that the airport would likely be a priority Russian target, they found themselves facing only two understrength National Guard company tactical groups, some 200 men in all. The brigade was newly raised and organized to NATO standards. However, most of its men, along with the brigade's complement of drones, light armour, and artillery, was closer to Kyiv. This force was largely made up of newly raised conscripts and rear-echelon troops, with only a couple of BTR-60 APCs. They had not even managed to establish strong defensive positions, not least because the managers from Antonov, who owned the airport, had reportedly kept them out until the day before: some darkly claim conspiracy, other suggest it was simply that they wanted to avoid the facility becoming a combat zone. Instead, the soldiers had been ordered to dig makeshift two-to-four person fighting positions.

While the Russians had not had the time to rehearse the specifics of the attack, they had detailed intelligence from both satellite surveillance and agents on the ground and were well-trained for such insertions. The Ukrainians put up a tough fight notwithstanding, but were soon running low on ammunition and withdrew in good order from their cantonment and out of the airport. They claim not to have suffered any fatalities, and although this was disputed by the Russians, no evidence of soldiers killed has even been presented. The squad left guarding the radar, though, was encircled and forced to surrender, making these the first prisoners of the war.

In any case, despite taking losses, Pankov's paratroopers were able to seize the airport by 1300, although they would continue to exchange sporadic fire with remaining Ukrainian troops of the 4th Op Bde. Without armoured vehicles or heavy weapons, and with the gunships headed back to Belarus, they lacked the capacity to move beyond the airport's perimeter in pursuit, especially as the National Guardsmen would be reinforced by armed local volunteers, as well as a platoon landed by an Mi-8 helicopter to the southwest of the airport. This was variously described as coming from the 80th Airborne Assault Bde or the 3rd Indep Special Operations Rgt.

It was then a race against time: would the Russians be able to flood the bridgehead with heavier forces before the Ukrainians could rush reinforcements to the airport? The defenders had been caught off guard, and were also suffering from communications problems thanks to Russian EW. By shortly after 1200, though, reinforcements were already on the way: a battalion from the 4th Bde which had been based in Hostomel village, including at least a platoon of T-64BV tanks (modernized versions of a venerable Soviet design, with new sights and reactive armour), a couple of companies of mechanized infantry in BMP-2 IFVs from the regular army's 72nd Mech Bde, and a team from the SBU's elite Alpha Group. There were some skirmishes that afternoon, but, contrary to some reports, no real counterattack. Hearing Kyiv claim that the airport had already been recaptured, CNN's Matthew Chance drove to the airport and, assuming they must be Ukrainian, asked the heavily-armed soldiers guarding the gate, 'where are the Russians?' 'We are the Russians,' they replied. His footage showed the paratroopers in black-and-orange recognition armbands firmly in control, even as sporadic gunfire rang out. One of the civilian personnel at the airport, who were allowed to leave, asked one of their officers, 'will there be trouble again now? Are you going to bomb everything here now?' His comforting reply was, 'No, we have already done our job. Everything will be fine. Don't worry.'

3RD SPECIAL OPERATIONS REGIMENT

The 3rd Indep Special Operations Rgt, named for Prince Svyatoslav the Brave, is descended originally from the Soviet 10th *Spetsnaz* Bde, which was on Ukrainian soil when the USSR was disbanded and thus reverted to Kyiv's control. The new Ukrainian government was unable to maintain it at brigade strength, though, and in 1998 it was reformed as the smaller and more practical 1st Indep Special Purpose Rgt, then in 2000 redesignated as the 3rd. It played a significant role in the fighting in the Donbas in 2014–17, even though it dipped to little more than battalion strength, but was then brought up to close to establishment strength in time for the invasion. On February 24, 2022, the 'Medoid' (Honey Badgers) Tactical Group, operating FPV drones, was added to its order of battle.

HQ Coy
  Security Plt
Intelligence Coy
  Scout Plt
1st Special Purpose Tactical Group
2nd Special Purpose Tactical Group
3rd Special Purpose Tactical Group
'Medoid' Tactical Group
Fire Support Group
Sniper Plt
Communications Plt
Medical Coy
Logistics Coy

A screen grab from an official Russian Defence Ministry video showing paratroopers from the 11th Independent Guards Air Assault Brigade taking Antonov Airport. Note the white recognition patches and also the orange and black St George's ribbons. (Mil.ru, CC 4.0)

However, while the paratroopers had indeed done their job, the Russian command had failed to exploit this victory quickly enough. The expectation had been that the first reinforcements would come by air. Early that evening, though, as the Il-76s transports were on their way from Pskov, a two-hour flight, two Ukrainian Su-24Ms made low passes over the airport dropping FAB-500 500kg bombs on the runway. It was then further cratered by long-range 203mm 2S7 Pions, D-30 122mm field guns from the 4th Bde's artillery company in Horenka to the east, and the 72nd Bde's 152mm 2S3 self-propelled guns. The runway was thus unusable, and the Russian aircraft had to be redirected to Bobruysk in east-central Belarus. (Claims that one was shot down appear untrue.) The plan to use Hostomel as a shortcut into Kyiv was thus foiled – and while the 11th Bde BTG held the airport, this was now a trap for them, unless and until heavy reinforcements could reach them by land. Even that now looked unlikely. The complacent assumption had been that, with mechanized forces crossing the Belarus border at 0400 and having only some 130km to cover, they would be at Hostomel before the evening. That would turn out, as discussed below, to be a generous and unrealistic estimate.

As night fell, the Ukrainians launched a proper attack, under the 72nd Bde's Col. Oleksandr Vdovychenko. Mi-24P and Mi-8 helicopters led the way for the ground troops, suppressing the paratroopers with salvos of S-8 80mm rockets. By this point, they had also been reinforced by a sniper team from the 'Shaman' Special Operations Bn, part of military intelligence (HUR) and elements from the 80th and 95th Indep Airborne

THE HOSTOMEL ASSAULT

Morning, 24 February, 2022. As Ka-52 and Mi-24 attack helicopters from the 440th Independent Guards Helicopter Regiment peel off to suppress the limited AA defences at the north end of the airport with rocket and cannon fire, Mi-8AMTSh assault helicopters prepare to insert Spetsnaz commandos and paratroopers from the 11th Independent Guards Air Assault Brigade to the south, where the main force of defenders is based, many dispersed into small dugouts. The runway has been blocked off with trucks, a fire engine, and a fuel tanker, but this poses no impediment to the helicopters. Already one of the twin-rotor Ka-52s is launching 80mm S-8 rockets from its underwing pods, followed by its wingman, while the lead Mi-24P loses altitude so as to bring the fixed twin 23mm cannon on the right-hand side of its fuselage to bear. Smoke from a previous rocket strike billows into the sky.

The Shaman Battalion is a HUR special forces unit officially established right before the invasion, although some claim it dates back to 2011. It specializes in sabotage and reconnaissance mission and, as the masks show, enjoys its reputation for unpredictable mayhem. (DIUfrogman, CC 4.0)

Assault Bdes. Paratroopers and special forces excel in rapid, unconventional operations, and can prove fragile when forced to fight an essentially defensive fight against enemy mechanized units with artillery support, and from positions which offer only limited cover. In hard fighting, including rocket strikes from a MiG-29 from the 40th Tactical Aviation Bde flying at rooftop height, the lightly armed Russians were pushed back into forests around the airport, with perhaps two thirds of their number by then dead or wounded. They had, after all, been almost entirely unsupported, bar a sortie by two Su-25 ground attack aircraft.

The next day, at around 1100, Russian ground forces, coordinating with another helicopter assault, would sweep back into the airport almost unopposed, as Ukrainian troops were withdrawn to Hostomel and Kyiv. Moscow would claim that 200 helicopters were involved in the assault – a wholly implausible claim, disputed by observers on the scene, who saw no more than 20–30 – but the deciding factor was really the ground advance. Later in the afternoon of the 24th, advanced elements of the reinforced 35th Combined Arms Army under Lt. Gen. Alexander Sanchik had powered through the Chernobyl Exclusion Zone and had reached the town of Ivankiv, and while the bulk of this column pressed on towards Kyiv, a BTG from the 31st Indep Guards Airborne Assault Bde was instead diverted to Hostomel.

The fight for the town

Around 1400hrs on 25 February, the Russian defence ministry announced their capture of Antonov Airport, but by then this was a rather empty victory given that the runway would have to be extensively repaired before it could be used. Although some remedial work would be done in the

THE CAPTURE OF CHERNOBYL

The Chernobyl (Chornobyl in Ukrainian) Nuclear Power Plant, site of a catastrophic meltdown in 1986, was undergoing decommissioning at the time of the invasion and was, as now, at the heart of the Chernobyl Exclusion Zone, a 2,600 square km region that is still one of the more radioactive in the world. Being on the Belarusian border and on the P56 highway into Ukraine, though, it was a logical waystation on the initial advance route.

It was protected by the 1st Nuclear Power Plant Defence Bn of the National Guard's 28th State Facilities Protection Rgt, but this 169-man unit was not equipped for serious combat operations so much as plant security. At around 1400 on 24 February, Russian Spetsnaz in Tigr LMVs arrived at the power station and soon negotiated its surrender, along with that of the 1st Bn. Moscow formally returned the power plant to Ukrainian control on 31 March.

coming weeks, it was not brought up to a standard which would accept heavy-lift transports, even if any could have safely penetrated Ukrainian airspace by that time.

In any case, on 26 February, the Russians turned to the town itself, which was defended primarily by the 4th Bde. First, the attackers moved almost unopposed into the so-called 'military settlement' by the airport. Formerly a garrison base, it had been converted largely into housing for Antonov workers and their families,

and most of its inhabitants had been sheltering in basements. As follow-on forces of Rosgvardiya, including Chechen fighters of the infamous 141st Special Motorised Rgt, arrived, checkpoints were set up and martial law imposed. (Whereas most regular army units deployed as BTGs generated by brigades or divisions, the 141st Rgt seems to have operated as a single unit.)

Then, the Russians established positions alongside the T1002 road that ran parallel to the Irpin River to the east, down through Hostomel, and into the adjacent town of Bucha that would later become infamous as the site of a massacre of civilians. They took the village of Chervonye to the north (where there was a bridge across the Irpin), and a field hospital and ammunition dump outside the village of Lubyanka to the west of the airport. Taking Hostomel itself would prove harder. By the 27th, while a separate force was attacking Bucha to the south, the BTG from the 31st Rgt was pushing into the town. As they were under observation by Ukrainian drones, the defenders were ready for them. Fighting concentrated around the crossroads of Svyato-Pokrovska Street and Buchanske Highway near the

The small defence unit still based at the Chernobyl Nuclear Power Plant had no choice but to surrender when faced with the vanguard of a whole army of Russian troops. (Getty)

The Chechen Kadyrovtsy like this SOBR officer from the 141st Special Motorized Regiment made much of its eagerness and military prowess, but acquired an unsavoury reputation amongst the rest of the Russian forces for its brutality and disinclination to engage in hard fighting. (Getty)

sprawling Vetropak glass factory, whose warehouses and industrial units proved a useful base for the defenders. The 31st Bde was mounted in a mix of BMD-2s and BMD-3s. The BMD is a compact 'pocket' IFV designed to be readily air-liftable and even able to be dropped by parachute, yet at the expense of size (it can just about carry three to four extra men in its cramped troop compartment) and protection. While both mount a stabilized 30 mm 2A42 autocannon, a 7.62 mm PKT coaxial machine gun, and a pintle-mount for an anti-tank missile launcher (though in practice this is often left off), the BMD-3 is slightly larger and more powerful. Both, though, make dangerous compromises to remain air-droppable, and their relatively thin aluminium armour provides little protection against heavy machinegun fire, let alone missiles and RPGs. A number would be destroyed as soon as they were deployed into the town, along with some of the heavier BMD-4s mounting a 100 mm 2A70 low-pressure rifled gun, which were being used for fire support, so the paratroopers took largely to attacking on foot. Even so, by the Russian withdrawal at the end of March, their confirmed losses would include more than 30 AFVs, mainly BMDs, but including some BMP-2s of the 141st Rgt as well.

After all, the Chechens would also take heavy losses, especially when a full company was caught in the open and strafed by rockets from Mi-24s on 1 March. Ukrainian claims that they deployed 250 AFVs and more than 1,500 of the 'best fighters of the Chechen Republic' need to be taken with as much scepticism as the subsequent ones of hundreds of casualties and 56 tanks destroyed (not least because the Russians did not deploy that many in the operation). Nonetheless, it is clear that the fighting was heavy and in the first few days alone, the 31st Bde lost at least 34 men, including the BTG commander, Maj. Alexei Osokin, but not Lt. Col. Magomed Tushayev,

141ST SPECIAL MOTORIZED REGIMENT

Technically the 141st Special Motorized Regiment, named after Hero of the Russian Federation A. A. Kadyrov, or more prosaically Military Unit 4156, this unit is part of the Rosgvardiya's Indep Order of Zhukov Op Purpose Bde, but its real loyalties are to Ramzan Kadyrov. Raised almost exclusively of Chechens and based at Grozny, the Chechen capital, it is one of the key units of *Kadyrovtsy* forming the basis of Kadyrov's power. Originally established as the 248th Special Motorized Battalion 'North' in 2006, during the mopping-up stage of the Second Chechen War, it was expanded and converted into the 141st Rgt in 2009. Since 2017 it had been led by Lt. Col. Magomet Tushayev, a hard-line Kadyrov loyalist. With a strength of 787 men, it includes an oversized reconnaissance company and mortar and air defence batteries. The unit has an infamous reputation for brutality, and would be implicated in the murder of civilians in neighbouring Bucha.

HQ
1st Motorized Bn (BMP-2)
2nd Motorized Bn (Ural-63095 APC, trucks)
3rd Motorized Bn (Ural-63095 APC, trucks)
Tank Coy (T-72)
Recon Coy
Sniper Plt
Mortar Bty
Grenade Launcher Plt (Tigr-M LMVs with AGS-17)
AD Bty
Engineer Plt
Communications Plt
Logistics Coy

commander of the 141st Rgt, whose death was alleged but later disproved. Indeed, some reports suggest that Maj. Gen. Andrei Sukhovetsky, the deputy commander of the 41st Combined Arms Army, was killed by a sniper while leading from the front in Hostomel, although others have placed his death elsewhere. Either way, he was the first general-rank officer killed in the war.

Nonetheless, by 5 March the defenders had been pushed out of all but the south-western outskirts of the town. On 8 March, the Russians switched tactics and launched a night-time attack on the remaining Ukrainian holdouts. However, this was only partly successful, especially as it led to several cases of near misses to friendly fire, and at least one fatality. By 11 March, the town was fully in Russian control, and *Kadyrovtsy* were reportedly terrorizing the remaining locals, even as Zelensky awarded Hostomel the honorific title of Hero City of Ukraine. Indeed, on 14 March, Kadyrov himself claimed to have visited his troops there, although no credible evidence of this was ever produced. Much like seizing the airport, though, this was something of a Pyrrhic victory, as the offensive against Kyiv had ground to an ignominious halt. The Ukrainians continued to assay counterattacks, on 16 and 20 March, that saw them briefly break back into Hostomel before being forced to withdraw under aerial bombardment. Those attacks may have been repelled, but the overall momentum of the war in the north had begun swinging Kyiv's way: by 1 April, the Russians were pulling out of Hostomel as Moscow reoriented its war towards the east.

A Ukrainian soldier atop a BTR-60PB APC celebrates the liberation of Hostomel. (Getty Images)

However, Russia's Hostomel operation could easily have had a much more serious effect on the Ukrainian command structure. In April 2023, Ukraine's then-Defence Minister Oleksii Reznikov noted that the official protocol in case of an attack on Kyiv had been for him and his team to relocate to a secure command bunker outside the city. In his words:

> The command post that was assigned to my staff was located, you'll laugh, in Hostomel, in a protected place that was amongst the first to be taken. Theoretically, if we had moved there, in at least a day or two, I would have had half of the ministry there.

The T-80BVM is an upgraded version of the T-80BV intended to bridge the gap between the T-80 and the most advanced tank in Russian service, the T-90M, with a new 125mm gun, as well as Relikt (explosive reactive armour), and improved optics. It has proven controversial, as many users complain that the supposed improvements simply add complexity and more things to break down. (Mil.ru, CC 4.0)

Fortunately for Reznikov, even as preparations were being made for the transfer, news came in about the assault on Hostomel, so they instead relocated to alternative defence ministry properties in Kyiv. The irony is that there is no evidence that Moscow knew of this plan, but under other circumstances, many of the most senior figures within the Ukrainian defence ministry, their files and their secure systems, might have been captured by just 300 paratroopers.

Battle and bloodletting in Bucha

While the Russians were continuing to try and secure Hostomel, they had also reached past it into another town whose name would become infamous: Bucha. A stepping-stone along the M07 highway on the way to Kyiv, Bucha was again expected to be a relatively easy capture, opening the way to

Irpin. Instead, it would see the invaders again bogged down in vicious street-to-street fighting with a mix of Ukrainian regulars, initially from the National Guard's 4th 'Rubizh' Bde, and local volunteers, which would culminate in a massacre of civilians that remains one of the low points even by the standards of this thoroughly brutal war.

A stray Rosgvardiya unit had passed through Bucha on 25 February, but it was not until two days later that the Russians made a serious advance on the town itself. A BTG of the 64th Indep Guards Motor Rifle Bde of the Eastern Military District's 35th Army led the way, a recently upgraded unit equipped with modernized T-80BVM tanks and heavily armed BMP-3 IFVs. It was supported by elements from the 234th Guards Air Assault Rgt and some of the more notorious Rosgvardiya troops, *Kadyrovtsy*, from the 249th Indep Special Motorized Bn 'South' and possibly also the 'Akhmat' Special Rapid-Response Detachment (SOBR).

As civilians tried desperately to flee to Kyiv, Bucha came under bombardment by mortars and heavier artillery. Buildings were damaged and the town's infrastructure quickly began to falter, with whole neighbourhoods losing water and power supplies. The Russians, under the 64th Bde's Col. Azatbek Omurbekov, began to advance into the town from Hostomel along Vokzalna Street, but this initial move was met by both locals throwing Molotov cocktails (setting at least one vehicle on fire) and a sustained barrage of long-range artillery fire. Vokzalna cuts through Bucha to neighbouring Irpin, and fearing that the attackers were really intending simply to roll through it, the bridge across the Bucha River connecting them was blown up later on the afternoon of the 27th.

At first, the Russians were hampered both by their concentration on one narrow entry point into the town and an apparent unwillingness to take

234TH GUARDS AIR ASSAULT REGIMENT

The 234th Rgt has a combat pedigree as long as its full official title: the 234th Guards Black Sea Airborne Assault Order of Kutuzov 3rd Degree Rgt, named after Alexander Nevsky. Established in 1926 as a regular line unit, the 221st Rifle Rgt of the 74th Taman Rifle Div, it became the 157th Rifle Div's 348th Rifle Rgt in 1939. It fought through the Second World War, being renamed the 234th Rifle Rgt and gaining the 'guards' honorific for its tenacious defence of Stalingrad. In 1946, it became a paratrooper unit, being redeployed to Pskov and joining the 76th Guards Airborne Div. It has taken part in every military deployment of the post-Soviet Russian army, from peacekeeping in the former Yugoslavia to the Chechen, Georgian, Ukrainian, and even Syrian wars. Now, while including a parachute-assault Bn mounted in a mix of BMD light IFVs and LMVs, it is essentially deployed by land or by helicopter.

HQ Coy
1st Airborne Assault Bn (BMD-2/3/4)
2nd Airborne Assault Bn (BMD-2/3/4)
Parachute-Assault Bn (BMD-2/3/4, Tigr LMV)
SPG Artillery Div (2S9 Nona-S gun-mortars)
1st AT Bty (BTR-RD Robot)
2nd AT Bty (2S25 Sprut-SD)
AA Bty (BTR-ZD Skrezhet)
Recon Coy (1V119 Reostat)
Engineer and Sapper Coy
Communications Coy
Airborne Support Coy
Logistics Coy
Repair Coy
NBC Protection Plt

Two Ukrainian snipers in ghillie suits seen during the fighting outside Brovary. The soldier on the left carries a Dragunov SVD, the one on the right a Zbroyar Z-008. (Photo by Andrii Kotliarchuk/ Getty Images)

casualties. As one Ukrainian military observer noted, 'had the [Russians] been willing to lose a company of tanks to force the way, they would have taken the bridge before anyone could do anything about it, and their first wave would probably have outrun the artillery,' as on that first day, the Ukrainian guns were firing blind, without any observers on the ground, or at least none that could talk to them, as EW was jamming radios and no one had yet thought of turning to civilians as spotters in this particular instance. Nonetheless, Omurbekov was cautious and while some more gung-ho airborne units from the 234th Rgt were subsequently able to reach Irpin, a quick seizure of Bucha turned into a slow and vicious battle.

The Russians repeatedly, in a massive breach of their own training and doctrine, launched armoured attacks without adequate infantry cover. In part this was because, deployed with little warning and without a general mobilization, many of the BTG's personnel carriers were crewed but lacked their full complements of infantry. One mechanized company, for example, was deployed with all 11 BMPs, but only half the infantry dismounts it should have had. The result was that, in Bucha's streets, they were very vulnerable not just to military anti-tank weapons but even Molotov cocktails and similar improvised weapons.

Over the next few days, the Russians would succeed in expanding a bridgehead in the town, but suffered significant losses, including over a

dozen tanks and IFVs. Nor were they always that impressive in the attack: in one incident, a Russian tank opened fire on what it thought was a Ukrainian armoured car, but proved to be an old BRDM-2 long since repurposed to be the town's memorial to the fallen in the Soviet invasion of Afghanistan (1979–88). In the early days, with most Ukrainian forces in the area focused on the immediate defence of Kyiv and the battles along other routes, reinforcements for Bucha were often few and drawn from a number of available reserves, including elements from the Azov Rgt and the National Guard's 1st 'Burevii' Bde.

By 2 March, there was a sense of greater organization to the defence, as the frontline had been held and the 331st stabilized. Humanitarian aid for the remaining civilians began to arrive, and on the 3rd, evacuations began, as regular units from the Ukranian Army began to push the Russians back away from the railway lines which bisect Bucha from southwest to northeast, raising their flag on the town administration building on Energetykiv Street. The defenders even began to hope that they could drive the attackers out of Bucha altogether.

In response, though, the Russians began to call in more reinforcements, while also stepping up their bombardment of the city, as well as calling in low-level rocket and bombing runs by Su-25s from the 899th Assault Aviation Rgt. By 7 March, paratroopers from the 104th and 234th Guards Air Assault Rgts, part of the 76th Guards Air Assault Div, and the 331st Guards Airborne Rgt, part of the 98th Guards Airborne Div, had joined

The sturdy Su-25 Grach (Rook) ground attack aircraft is a mainstay of both the Russian and Ukrainian air fleets, mounting a 30mm Gryazev-Shipunov GSh-30-2 autocannon and able to carry 8,000kg of ordnance on 11 hardpoints. (Getty)

the attack, and were poised in three assault groups ready to attack from the north and west. Artillery bombardment started fires at NII SV, the Research Institute of Glass and Ceramics, sending toxic smoke billowing into the sky. Over the next couple of days, the Russians slowly ground forwards, and on 9 March, a further, major evacuation of civilians marked a sense on the defenders' side that the tide had turned against them.

On 12 March, the local administration announced that the city had fallen. Although there would be a limited attempt at a counterattack on the 16th, Bucha would remain in Russian hands until troops were pulled out at the end of the month as part of the wider withdrawal from the Kyiv offensive. When government forces returned to Bucha, they found a scene of carnage. While some Russians had maintained their discipline and treated the civilians left in Bucha with a modicum of restraint – even while looting their homes, especially for food, as the limited supplies they had been issued at the start of the operation had been exhausted – others had descended into brutality and atrocity. The Chechen National Guardsmen had primary responsibility for rear area security and they took this as carte blanche to harass, torture and murder with impunity while launching their *zachistka* 'clean-up' operations. Alongside some of the regular troops, they engaged in what were arguably the worst abuses of the war (as of writing). There had been civilian deaths from artillery due to simply being caught in the crossfire, but what emerged was a story of systematic killings: of civilians tortured for information, beaten, and executed. To this day it is impossible to say for sure how many were deliberately killed in this way rather than being the depressingly usual collateral casualties of war: the estimates range from over a hundred to maybe five times that.

Moscow claimed that this was all lies or a Ukrainian 'false flag' operation to discredit it, despite the copious amounts of physical evidence and testimony collected by the UN Commissioner for Human Rights and investigators from the International Criminal Court. In a clear message of defiance, on 13 July 2022, Putin made Omurbekov, who had subsequently been wounded, a Hero of the Russian Federation, Russia's highest military award, but in a secret ceremony, before he was transferred out of field command, to head the 392nd Regional Training Centre. Omurbekov had a poor enough reputation before Bucha – when, right before the invasion, some of his men expressed a desire not to participate, he reportedly hit one in the face with a rifle butt, and put his service pistol against another's temple, saying 'I will shoot you right now and get away with it' – but when news of his award broke, even a commentator on an army social media channel wondered 'what is he going to teach people? How to hide in a cellar and order people to gun down civvies?'

The drive on Kyiv

The real prize was, of course, Kyiv, as both the practical and symbolic heart of the Ukrainian state that Putin was so determined to tame.

The plan had been for a sudden, dramatic blitzkrieg that would see Russian troops at the city's outskirts, if not further, on the first day, and its full encirclement and capture within three. After all, it was only 125km by road from the border to Kyiv: what could go wrong? Much, of course, did, and it soon became clear that – again, in contravention of doctrinal precepts – there were no alternative plans ready in case the initial advances bogged down. Operational and field commanders were forced to improvise as best they could, often tripping each other up, while Moscow constantly and impotently demanded consistent and quicker progress. As one major from the 64th Indep Motor Rifle Bde complained with more vigour than political correctness, the NTsUO, under pressure from the Kremlin, had 'simply become a nagging wife, shouting at her husband to get his work done sooner.'

A Russian T-80BVM tank and BMP-2 IFVs pass a row of trucks, all marked with the V recognition symbol, during the infamous drive of the 'armoured traffic jam' towards Kyiv at the start of March. (Mil.ru, CC 4.0)

The two columns intended to take Kyiv, from Belarus to the northwest and Bryansk in Russia from the northeast, set off around 0400hrs on 24 February. As already mentioned, the former, largely built around 10 BTGs drawn from the 35th Combined Arms Army and the paratroopers of 31st Indep Guards Air Assault Bde had crossed through the Chernobyl Exclusion Zone and reached Ivankiv, north of Kyiv, by late afternoon. This was crucial, because it held a bridge across the Teteriv River, and also access to the P02 highway to Kyiv.

The siege of Chernihiv

The operational group charged with attacking Kyiv from the northeast numbered some 30,000 men in BTGs largely drawn from the Central Military District. This is the direction from which Ukraine's high command expected the thrust to come, and against it was arrayed the

1st Tank Bde, headquartered at Honcharivske, 35km southwest of Chernihiv. The brigade's base was hit by missiles in the initial Russian strike early on the 24th, but its commander, Col. Leonid Khoda, had already ordered the force to disperse for this very reason, and while some buildings were damaged and some stores destroyed, its combat strength was intact. The initial plan was for the 1st Bde to deploy along a 45km defensive line between Ripky, 35km northwest of Chernihiv up the E95 highway, and Horodnya, 55km northeast, up the P13. However, by the time the Ukrainians had reformed after their dispersal, the fast-moving Russian advance forces had already reached and passed both towns. Instead, it was only at Velyki Osniaky and Sedniv, on the E95 and P13 respectively, halfway to Chernihiv, that a combination of the 1st Bde's vanguard and local territorial defence forces were able to engage them.

These were, however, ambushes and brief skirmishes able to do little more than force the Russians briefly to pause and slow their overall advance. Only at the village of Khaliavyn, just 6km north of the city's limits, was there the first real engagement, late in the afternoon of the first day of the war. This was a wooded area, and, in the short-range meeting engagements, the upgraded 2017-model Ukrainian T-64s were more than able to hold their own against the more modern Russian tanks thanks to their faster autoloaders (which meant they could fire more often), more capable sights, and the way the terrain prevented the attackers from exploiting their superior numbers.

Nonetheless, the unexpected resistance of the 1st Bde and local militias and territorial defence units – some of whom had modern AT systems such as the domestic Stuhna-P (alternatively Stugna-P or Skif) laser-beam riding missile and NLAWs – made the Russians think twice about the plan to roll straight into Chernihiv. There, the 1st Bde would be supported by

1ST TANK BRIGADE

Ukraine's 1st 'Siverska' Tank Bde was formed in 1997 from the former 292nd Tank Rgt of the 72nd Mech Div, which was being dissolved. In 2022, it comprised some 2,000 troops and more than 100 tanks, all variants of the T-64. Elements of the brigade took part in the undeclared war in the Donbas, fighting at Luhansk in 2014 and Debaltseve in 2015.

HQ Coy (Honcharivske)
  Signal Coy
1st Tank Bn (T-64BV)
2nd Tank Bn (T-64BM)
3rd Tank Bn (T-64BM)
4th Tank Bn (T-64B)
1st Mech Bn (BMP-1/2)
1st Motorized Bn

2nd Motorized Bn
Artillery Group
  HQ Bty
  1st Arty Div (122mm 2S1 Gvozdika SPG)
  2nd Arty Div (152mm 2S3 Akatsiya SPG)
  3rd Arty Div (BM-21 Grad MLRS)
  AT Bn (100mm MT-10 Rapira)
AA Bn
Recon Coy
Engineer Bn
Maintenance Bn
Logistic Bn
Radar Coy
Medical Coy
Chemical, Biological, Radiological, and Nuclear
    Defence Coy

the infantry of the 114th Territorial Defence Bde and also elements of the 58th Motorized Bde. This had originally deployed between the towns of Baturyn and Hlukhiv to the east to block the M02 highway into Chernihiv. Faced with superior Russian forces, it retreated first to Konotop, and then the southern periphery of Chernihiv. For commanders who still had vivid memories of the terrible losses suffered when Russian armoured forces attacked the city of Grozny during the two Chechen wars (1994–96 and 1999–2009), the thought of getting bogged down in urban fighting for what was not their primary objective made little sense.[3] Instead, by late on 25 February, the main invading force was bypassing the city, taking the E95 highway to the west. They left behind a detachment initially made up of BTGs from the 35th and 74th Indep Guards Motor Rifle Bdes to besiege Chernihiv, as much to contain the 1st Bde as necessarily to take it.

For six weeks, the Russians kept up their siege, although after an initial and abortive attempt to rush the city on 26 February by the 35th Bde which took heavy casualties from mines and RPGs, it was often characterized by more air and artillery attacks instead of direct attacks on the ground. BM-21 and 220mm BM-27 Uragan MLRSs were especially used to bombard the centre of the city, but while there were sporadic attempts to break through the defensive line, such as an attack by what seems to have been a reinforced company of the 74th Bde on the 28th, the Russians seemed reluctant to engage fully, again demonstrating an aversion to the inevitable high losses that they would have taken.

Only on 3 March, with the arrival of a fresh BTG from the 55th Guards Mountain Motor Rifle Bde, famed for its toughness, was a serious attack

A T-64BM Bulat, a distinctive Ukrainian modernization of the T-64. This T-64BM mounts Nizh explosive reactive armour and a new 125mm KBA3 gun with TO1-KO1ER night sight. However dated the original T-64 design, the Bulat proved an effective tank, especially in the short-range tank duels that often characterized the early stage of the war (Photo by MAJ Neil Penttila/7th Army Training Command Public Affairs, CC 2.0)

3 See ESS 78 *Russia's Wars in Chechnya 1994–2009*

Ukrainian soldiers prepare a Stuhna-P AT missile launcher. (Getty)

launched. Although the bridge over the Desna River, south of Chernihiv, had been destroyed, the Russians spanned it with a PP-2005 pontoon bridge and, despite efforts to destroy it with artillery fire, then used that to assault the village of Yahidne. With Su-25 aircraft providing close air support, Yahidne was quickly taken, and on 5 March, the Russians began to probe Ivanivka, the next village along the M01 road to Chernihiv. They faced two depleted platoons from the 58th Motorized Bde: some 50 effective and five dated BMP-1 IFVs, which were quickly swept away, all the BMPs being destroyed. Nonetheless, they had bought the Ukrainians some time, and by the time the Russians tried to move on to Kolychivka, the next village along the M01, on 6 March, a more serious defence had been prepared. A company of 58th Bde tanks, supported by a company of infantry and as many National Guard were able to prevent any further advance, even if one Russian push did make it to the centre of the village, to be confronted with a barricade of buses, emplaced tanks, and SPG-9 recoilless rifles.

Meanwhile, the city itself was coming under increasingly heavy air attack, as Su-25 and larger Su-34 'Fullback' striker aircraft, as well as Su-24 bombers from the 2nd Bomber Aviation Rgt delivered FAB-500 high explosive and OFZAB-500 incendiary 'dumb' (unguided) bombs that rained on military and civilian targets alike. Combined with the regular rocket and artillery strikes, they shattered the city's infrastructure and led to substantial civilian casualties: on 16 March, for example, a breadline came under attack, killing at least 18 and injuring another 26. Many fled, and by

The 220mm BM-27 Uragan (Hurricane) can deliver mines, cluster munitions and HE rounds to a range of 35km. This example is fielded by the 165th Artillery Brigade, which was attached to the 'V' group of forces. (Mil.ru, CC 4.0)

10 March, when Mayor Vladyslav Atroshenko claimed that the city was wholly surrounded, around half Chernihiv's 300,000 people had left. Even then, though, there was still a narrow 'road of life' through which supplies were brought in for most of the siege. The Russians failed to sever – or even apparently notice – a supply line into the city via a small road through the village of Anysiv to the southeast, until 25 March.

Nonetheless, through March no serious attempt was made to storm Chernihiv, especially as Moscow began to realize that its northern campaign as a whole was unlikely to succeed. On 31 March, Ukrainian forces were able to reopen the road to the city and break the siege, almost without a shot fired, as the Russians were already preparing to withdraw, something which became evident the next day. There were continued clashes as the Russians conducted a fighting retreat, but by 5 April, they had abandoned the whole Chernihiv Region.

Some credit Chernihiv's resistance with stymying the Russian advance from the northeast, and even though most of the invaders bypassed the city, it certainly did tie up men and resources that could conceivably have helped in the drive on Kyiv. Either way, it had soon become clear that if either of the two main thrusts was going to reach and take the capital, it would be Sanchik's from the northwest. It was almost twice the size of Lapin's force, after all, and initially only seemed to face a single Ukrainian brigade, and an under-strength one at that.

The 72nd to the defence

The primary unit deployed for the initial protection of Kyiv was the 72nd 'Black Zaporozhians' Mech Bde. A capable, but under-strength unit, it was also hobbled by a lack of clear intelligence about precisely which route the Russians might take. The assumption had been that the main attack would come east of the Dnipro, through Chernihiv. Nonetheless, they fortunately recognized the possibility of an attack from the northwest, too, but this did mean that the brigade was forced to spread itself in a 70km semicircle around about half the city's perimeter, from the village of Stoyanka in the west to the suburb of Brovary in the east. The main concentration of forces was to the northeast, with the brigade's 1st and 3rd Mech Bns, 1st and 3rd Artillery Divs (rather confusingly, the Ukrainian and Russian militaries both use the term 'division' also as an intermediate artillery structure usually comprising two or four 4-gun batteries), most of the 100mm AT guns of the 4th Div, and the lion's share of support elements. The 12th Bn, a former VTO unit added to the brigade's complement, remained in the capital itself.

Given the planning assumption that any attack from the northwest would be lighter, possibly just a diversion, defending against it was just the 2nd Bn, supported by the 2nd Artillery Div and a battery each of MT-12 Rapira AT guns and BM-21 Grad MLRSs. They were largely strung along a 22km line from just east of Bucha, to Horenka on the E373 highway, across to Lyutizh on the P02 highway, and to the western bank of the Dnipro. Considering that the 2nd Bn was the most depleted of the brigade's main formations, this meant that the defences to the northwest were dangerously thin, but it was assumed that they would not face a serious threat and that, if anything, their longer-ranged 152mm 2S3 guns would be called on to provide fire support for the rest of the brigade.

The 2nd Bn's 4th Coy was assigned to the defence of Horenka and the E373 road into Kyiv; the 5th Coy was sent to secure the village of Moshchun in the woods north of Horenka and a swathe of land to the west, towards

THE 72ND MECHANIZED BRIGADE

The history of the 72nd Mechanized Brigade, named after the Black Zaporozhians, dates back to the Second World War, having originally been the 29th Rifle Division, then the 72nd Guards Rifle Division, eventually transitioning from the Soviet to Ukrainian army. It played a significant role in the 2014 conflict in the Donbas and rotated there regularly from its cantonment in Bila Tserkva, 85km south of Kyiv. It had been due to do so again in late 2021, but had been held back to protect the capital as fears of an invasion grew. However, in part as a result, the brigade had not received a full allotment of replacements and so instead of its establishment strength of 3,000, it was at closer to 1,900 effective.

Brigade HQ (Bila Tserkva)
  Signal Coy
1st Mech Inf Bn (BMP-2)
2nd Mech Inf Bn (BMP-2)
3rd Mech Inf Bn (BMP-2)

12th Indep Motorized Infantry Bn 'Kyiv'
Tank Bn (T-64BV)
Mortar Bn (82mm and 120mm mortars)
Brigade Artillery Group
  HQ and Target Acquisition Coy
  1st Artillery Div (122mm 2S1 Gvozdika SPGs)
  2nd Artillery Div (152mm 2S3 Akatsiya SPGs)
  3rd Artillery Div (BM-21 Grad MRLS)
  4th Artillery Div (100mm MT-12 Rapira AT guns)
Air Defence Bn (9K35 Strela-10, Strela-2 and
  Igla MANPADS)
Engineer Bn
  Engineer Reconnaissance Plt
  Mining and De-mining Coy
Radio-Electronic Plt
Logistics Bn
Maintenance Bn
Radar Coy
Medical Coy

Hostomel, which was criss-crossed by irrigation channels; and the 6th Coy took the final portion of the defensive line, from Huta-Mezhyhirska north of Moshchun to Lyutizh. The battalion HQ was established at Pushcha-Vodytsya, to the southeast of Horenka, an urban settlement better known for its sanatoria and officials' residences, but surrounded by woods and home to a military hospital.

Reflecting the government's eleventh-hour realization that an invasion was imminent, the brigade only began to deploy from its base at Bila Tserkva

Ever since 2015, the sleeve patch of the 72nd Mechanized Brigade, named after the Black Zaporozhians, appropriately reads 'Ukraine or Death.' (President.gov.ua, CC 4.0)

The 2S1 Gvozdika (Carnation) 122mm self-propelled howitzer, as used by the 72nd Brigade's 1st Artillery Division, was originally developed in Soviet Ukraine, although since the influx of Western aid after the invasion, it is increasingly rare. (mil.gov. ua, CC 4.0)

south of the capital) on 22 February, two days before the attack. It was not the smoothest of processes, because while the soldiers had been preparing for a potential conflict for some months, the specific manoeuvre orders were hurriedly generated on the day. Because of a lack of transport, as well as a desire not to cause panic in the local population, brigade commander Col. Olexander Vdovichenko chose to move the 1st and 3rd Bns first. This meant that the 2nd Bn and 2nd Artillery Div only deployed in the early hours of the 24th, which was in the nick of time, both because the initial Russian move would come to the northwest of Kyiv and also because the base at Bila Tserkva was hit in the first wave of missile attacks that morning. By then, though, the 72nd was already on the move.

Hydraulic warfare

Meanwhile, so were the Russians, with just 125km along the P56 and P02 highways to cover. Nonetheless, like Lapin's column, they faced sporadic resistance as they punched through smaller towns and villages along the way. This again caused delays and generally instilled a greater caution. They were also suffering from Putin's refusal to let his generals know in good time what he planned. Most of the units were low on food and fuel, only having enough for a few days, lacked proper communications systems and, crucially, were unprepared for the tough winter conditions. Trucks lacked heavy, all-weather tyres, soldiers did not have warm enough clothing, and no consideration had been given to the fact that even when not moving they would keep their vehicles' engines idling to power the heating systems, further depleting their fuel supplies. Tanks and trucks venturing off the

Most Rosgvardiya, like these parading through Moscow in an KamAZ-435029 Patrul-A armoured vehicle, are riot police and security guards rather than combat soldiers, and suffered as a result when facing full-scale combat. (Presidential Administration of Russia, CC 3.0)

roads risked getting stuck in the mud, and where all-too-scarce recovery vehicles were unavailable, farmers were forced to help extricate them, often at gunpoint. (They would arguably have the last laugh, as later the sight of immobilized Russian vehicles being towed away by farmers back to the Ukrainian lines would become something of a meme.)

It was a sign of the chaos on the Russian side that one Rosgvardiya force, cut off from the main advance, even seems to have tried to rush Kyiv on its own. On 25 February, some 80 security troops from Kemerovo Region's National Guard contingent, a mix of OMON militarized riot police and SOBR police SWAT teams, mounted in a single BTR-60 APC and a mix of lightly armoured Ural-572060 trucks and unarmoured Ural-4320s, tried to reach the city limits along the M07 road north of Irpin. Having rolled through Bucha, they were ambushed on the bridge over the Irpin River with devastating effect. In a hail of machine-gun fire, rocket-propelled grenades, and even dated 9K111 Fagot (AT-4 Spigot) AT missile fire, every vehicle was destroyed and reportedly only three wounded men survived.

Nonetheless, that same day the advance elements of the main force reached Demydiv, some 30km from the city limits. They planned to press on, and would have, were it not for one inconvenient fact: the Irpin River which ran south of the township had burst its banks, and the irrigation channels which threaded through the farmland to south and east were also flooding, turning the fields into icy swampland that would bog down a tank or a truck. This was no random Act of God, though.

Hydraulic warfare would prove a crucial aspect of the defence of Kyiv, with bridges and waterways proving to be powerful constraints on the Russian advance. Many bridges were destroyed by demolition charges or artillery fire: the bridge over the Teteriv at Ivankiv, for example, and the Romanovka Bridge between Irpin and Kyiv. However, the most dramatic such operation was the breaching of the Kozarovychi (or Irpin) Dam on 25 February. Part of the Kyiv hydroelectric power system, the dam had been built at the junction of the Irpin and Dnipro Rivers, by the village of Kozarovychi, 22km north of the capital. This was part of the process of forming the Kyiv Reservoir in the 1960s, whose waters are 3m higher than the Irpin.

Based heavily on interviews on the ground, Sladden, Collins, and Connable have provided a detailed and evocative account of this operation, which also highlights the importance of volunteers and the initiative of experts in the civilian population in the defence of Ukraine. They recount how a businessman from Kyiv came up with the idea of breaching the dam to flood the northeast-flowing Irpin River and swathe of land alongside it threaded with irrigation canals. While one of his friends, a civilian videographer, inspected the dam both physically and via drone, he leveraged his contacts to secure a meeting with Col. Gen. Olexander Syrsky, the commander of Ukraine's army and the man in overall charge of the defence of Kyiv. He made his pitch, that if the dam were to be blown, then the narrow Irpin could be widened by more than a hundred metres, bridges might be swept away or inundated, roads drowned, and farmland turned into impassable

The 203mm 2S7 Pion (Peony) self-propelled howitzer, with its 38km range, provided the Ukrainians with valuable long-range firepower, even if it lacked the accuracy to deal with the sluice gate at Chervonye. (mil.gov.ua, CC 4.0)

swamp. Syrsky quickly agreed, especially as all that was being asked of him, beyond his blessing, was 'an engineer and some explosives.'

On the afternoon of the 25th, as the Russians were pushing past Demydiv to the east, raising the risk that they would be cut off, a team of civilian volunteers and their assigned sapper drove to the dam. The challenge was to blow a hole large enough to flood the Irpin, but not to destroy the dam altogether and with it the road along its 1.4km length, which refugees were still using to flee the Russian advance. At 1530hrs, the charges were set and detonated. As this was just a breach in the structure and not a catastrophic rupture, there was no cinematic wall of water roaring down the Irpin, but instead a steady flow that would eventually see 31 billion gallons of water flow into it, soon bursting its banks. Eventually, the level of the Irpin River as far as a sluice gate at Chervonye would rise by some 3m.

Those forces moving through Demydiv would soon be halted by the floods, at least until they could deploy pontoon bridges, but in many ways the crucial stretch of the river was precisely that further south. The intervention of that sluice gate was unexpected, as the hope had been that the swollen Irpin would also protect the western flank of the 72nd Bde's 2nd Bn. It was impossible to get personnel to it to open it, and attempts to destroy it by both cannon fire and 203mm shells from Pion 2S7 guns also failed.

The Russians were therefore able to bypass the flooded zones to the south, leading to the battle for Moshchun described below, building pontoon bridges along the newly swollen river. As a result, on 8 March, the army blew a much larger breach in the dam, releasing enough water to overwhelm the sluice gate and flood the next stage of the Irpin. By the end of the month, some 46 square km would be under water. Eventually, as the battle for Kyiv conclusively turned, the Zdvyzh and Teteriv Rivers further west were also flooded, in order to deny the Russians any viable route for retreat other than the P02 bridge at Ivankiv. Other units would assay even more circuitous routes, including one which swung to join the E40 Zhitomyr–Kyiv highway some 80km to the west, then the T1028 towards the township of Fastiv, southwest of the capital. A transport hub through which supply trains were still running to Kyiv, this was also regarded as a potential gateway to an attack on the capital from the south. As it was, this roundabout and tentative probe ended up turning back, as there were simply no forces available to reinforce it enough plausibly to be able to assault Fastiv, which was defended by the 208th Territorial Defence Bn.

The battle for Irpin

Unable to push directly south from Demydiv, the Russian advance guard looped round to the west to find new routes into Kyiv. On 26 February, a company-sized force launched a probing attack into the village of Stoyanka east of the city, along the E40 highway which spears into the centre of the capital. Approaching the bridge across the Irpin River there, they were engaged by elements of the 72nd Bde with tank fire and Javelin AT missiles. These were something of an unknown quantity still for the Ukrainian troops, as they had only just been issued and one officer interviewed by Sladden, Collins, and Connable explained just how new these were for them: 'Some units received training, but we did not... In my company, if a position had a Javelin, one soldier dug a hole while the other watched a YouTube video on how to fire it.' Nonetheless, they proved highly effective and helped repel the attack, after which engineers demolished this bridge, too.

THE FGM-148 JAVELIN

The US-made Javelin, an infrared-guided fire-and-forget anti-tank missile, first saw combat use in the 2003 war with Iraq, but has been steadily updated ever since and would prove highly effective in the initial fight against the armour-heavy Russian forces. With a range of 2.5 km or 4 km, depending on the model, its tandem-charge 8.4 kg warhead can defeat even explosive reactive armour and the missile can be set either for direct fire or a top-attack profile allowing it to plunge into a vehicle's thinner roof armour. The manufacturers, Lockheed Martin, claimed a 93% 'engagement success rate,' and indeed, 'Saint Javelin' – an image of the Virgin Mary holding a launcher – became one of the early symbols of Ukrainian resistance. No weapon is truly a 'silver bullet,' though, and subsequent more critical assessments suggest that, when one actually looks at vehicles knocked out rather than just hit, especially once the Russians had begun to adapt, including fitting so-called 'cope cages' of netting or metal slats above their vehicles to trigger warheads prematurely, the 'kill rate' was closer to 7% – although in terms of the arithmetic of modern warfare, that is still an impressive score.

A more significant advance was made along the T1002 road from Demydiv to Horenka, in the process skirting the areas in which, on the other side of the river, the 5th and 6th Coys of the 72nd Bde's 2nd Bn were deployed. As a result, the Russians were under constant observation, and had to run the gauntlet of harassing fire. Nonetheless, their objective was the substantial town of Irpin, to the east of beleaguered Bucha, and the nearby bridge to Horenka. While some fled Irpin, many residents established their own militias, outstripping the supply of weapons available. Makeshift bomb shelters were opened, checkpoints established, and even those unwilling or unable to fight were encouraged to pass on any sightings of the Russians to the defenders.

While Horenka was being pounded by artillery and kamikaze drones (including the very dangerous Lancet loitering munition), on 27 February, the Russians made their first move against Irpin, just before the Ukrainians blew the bridge linking it to Bucha, in effect making them two distinct combat zones. Russian forces moving into the town across the bridge were met by a VTO militia unit. It was able to use AT missiles to knock out the lead T-72B tank from the 4th Indep Motor Rifle Bde while it was still on the bridge, blocking it for long enough for the 152mm guns of the 72nd Bde's 2nd Artillery Div to be slewed round and shell the area. In due course, the Russians resumed their advance, and the Giraffe shopping centre became a particular focus of fighting: it was only two storeys high, but its location right by the Bucha River gave it a potentially commanding position. With the destruction of the bridge, though, the fighting shifted to the north of

Although Ukraine had been producing its own APCs such as the BTR-3 and BTR-4, the venerable Soviet BTR-60PB, for all its numerous faults, remained one of the mainstays of the Ukrainian forces in 2022, even if they have since been supplemented and often replaced by newer or better Western designs. (Getty)

the town. To get to it, the Russians – who at this stage were still unwilling to make dismounted assaults – had to cross relatively narrow stretches of open land between woods and the Irpin River, which became a killing zone for artillery and direct fire from the town.

The defenders were soon reinforced by a platoon of T-64BVs from the 2nd Bn and later a desperate collection of whatever troops were available, including a battalion of the Interior Ministry's newly formed 1st Special Purpose Police Assault Rgt 'Safari', a motorized light infantry force made up from a variety of police SWAT and bomb-disposal teams. Nevertheless, the Russians were able eventually to push into the margins of the town by early March. The Irpin Military Hospital in the northwest of the town and the nearby high-rise blocks of flats in the Irpenskie Lipki neighbourhood, which provided visibility and fire control over the surrounding area, were particular bones of contention, especially once the long-range Uragan MLRSs and 152mm 2S19 Msta-S SPGs of the 30th Artillery Bde were brought up to support the Russian attack.

As with so many of these individual attacks on the towns and villages around Kyiv, the Russians proved cautious and also were operating in small units, typically attacking with no more than a company – if that – at a time, and failing to follow their doctrine and pouring in more forces whenever they were able to secure a bridgehead. Even though most were paratroopers from 237th Guards Airborne Assault Rgt of the 76th Air Assault Div and the 173rd Indep Guards Recon Bn of the 106th Guards Airborne Div, considered to be among the Russian military's more aggressive and elite units, they made very heavy weather of advancing into the city. On 8 March, they relayed a demand for surrender to Olexander Markushyn, its mayor, who replied that 'Irpin

THE BATTLE FOR MOSHCHUN

The battle for Moschun – really only a skirmish – was typical of so many of the small-scale engagements played out through the invasion, in which probing attacks, on meeting resistance, would withdraw rather than push on at the risk of taking heavy casualties. With other routes across the Irpin River blocked, even the smallest bridge became a potential backdoor into Kyiv. The village of Moshchun, north of Horenka, was built by a narrow concrete one-lane bridge that was nonetheless strong enough to bear the weight of a tank. It was just part of the area assigned to the 2nd Coy of the 72nd Bde's 2nd Bn, only around 100 men with just five of the British-supplied NLAW AT missiles which were beginning to reach the front line. It was attacked on 27 February by a company of Russian paratroopers from the 234th Air Assault Rgt, mounted in 13 BMD-2 IFVs and one command vehicle. They had already crossed the river by the time they were engaged by a platoon of three BMP-2s, who were soon joined by Territorial Defence volunteers who had been assigned to the company. After a confused skirmish which left much of the village on fire, the Russians withdrew, abandoning their disabled command vehicle. There would be further clashes in Moshchun, including one attack by marines from the 155th Naval Inf Bde on 6 March, but the arrival of elements of the National Guard's 1st 'Bureviy' Presidential Op Bde named after Hetman Petro Doroshenko ensured that it was held until the bridge had been destroyed. Twice, the Russians then tried to lay pontoon bridges across the river, only to be spotted by drones and destroyed by artillery, until a third, successful attempt was made further downstream.

THE ATTACK ON KYIV

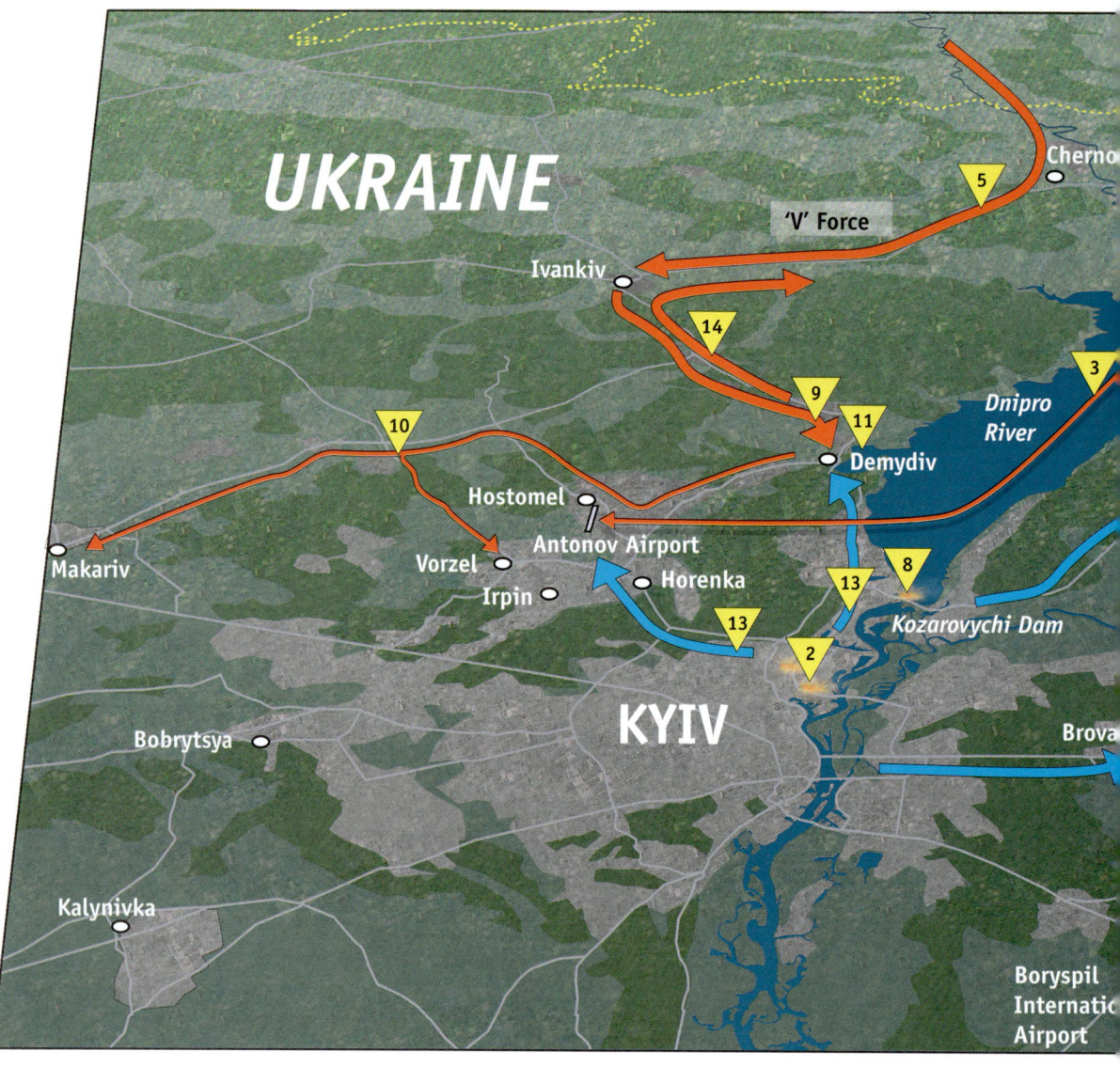

▼ EVENTS

24 February

1. Preliminary air and missile strikes across Ukraine.
2. Sabotage attacks in Kyiv.
3. Helicopter assault takes Antonov Airport
4. Ground assaults from Bryansk and Gomel.
5. 'V' force pushes through Chernobyl Exclusion Zone and reaches Ivankiv.
6. 'O' force sets off from Gomel and Bryansk Region.

25 February

7. 'O' force bypasses Chernihiv; begins siege.
8. Ukrainians breach Kozarovychi Dam.

26 February

9. 'V' force main body reaches Demydiv.

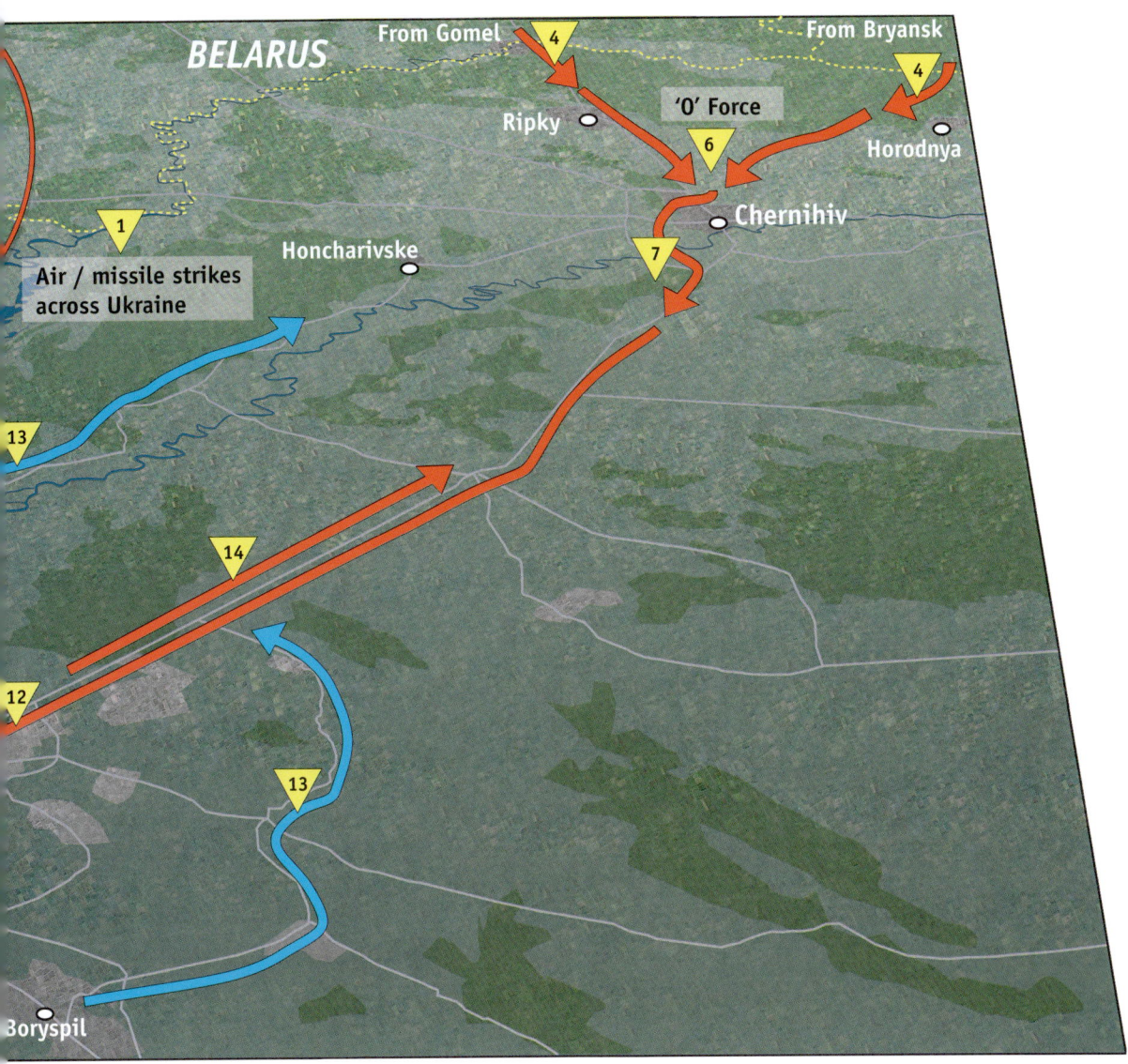

BELARUS

From Gomel

From Bryansk

Ripky

'O' Force

Horodnya

Chernihiv

Honcharivske

Air / missile strikes across Ukraine

Boryspil

27 February

10. 'V' force send out probes to east.

1 March

11. V' force main body stalls at Demydiv.

9 March

12. 'O' force main body reaches Brovary.

22 March

13. Ukrainians launch counterattack.

29 March

14. Russians begin to withdraw.

can't be bought, Irpin fights.' Nonetheless, the Russians were still taking Irpin, block by block and by 14 March, they controlled about half of it. On 20 March, though, the Ukrainian forces launched a counter-offensive in the Kyiv Region, and the Russian forces at Irpin faced the risk of being surrounded. They soon stopped making any attempts to move forward and began preparing to withdraw. On 28 March, Ukrainian forces began re-entering previously Russian-held sectors, and by the 30th Irpin had been fully liberated.

The heavily armoured traffic jam

So why were the Russian attacks so often uncoordinated, small scale, and brief? In part, this was a matter of poor planning. Convinced the Ukrainians would fold at the sight of Russian military might, Putin and his closest advisors did not plan or, crucially, arrange supply for an extended conflict. The General Staff, left to its own devices, would have prepared for all sorts of contingencies, but as it was, most of the commanders involved were scrambling at the last minute, and many of the units deployed with only a few days' food and fuel, with inadequate maps and very detailed orders which quickly became impossible to follow.

At the same time, even before they could mount any more substantial defence, the Ukrainians were harassing the armoured columns which were essentially confined to the roads because of the geography, the

A tank, whose camouflage is somewhat at odds with its bright Ukrainian colours drives though Irpin, being greeted by a relieved local. (Getty)

conditions, and their own need for speed. Gen. Valery Zaluzhny, the Ukrainian commander-in-chief, had settled precisely on a strategy of myriad smaller-scale attacks to deplete and slow the Russian advance while reserves were mustered. Bottlenecks were blocked by mines or improvised barricades, or became prime locations for ambushes, often making effective use of Stuhna-P AT missiles or else the growing stocks of US-supplied Javelins and the lighter British-supplied NLAWs. Although their value would soon wane as the Russians learned to jam or shoot them down, in the early months of the war, the Turkish-made Bayraktar TB2 medium-altitude long-endurance drones of the 383rd Indep Unmanned Aviation Complexes Rgt would also prove of great value, sometimes dropping ordnance but above all spotting for Ukrainian artillery. After all, while drones and AT missiles tend to get much coverage, artillery remained the primary means of inflicting casualties and destroying advancing vehicles.

Meanwhile, even an area of undoubted Russian excellence, electronic warfare (EW), was proving something of a disadvantage. With the battlespace so confused and Ukrainian forces launching ambushes and raids right across it, they were hesitant about moving their more advanced systems, like the truck-mounted Murmansk-BN jammer, across

If they could blow bridges when Russian forces were on them, then the Ukrainians did, as this trapped and ruined Russian tank at Kalynivka attests. (mvs.gov.ua, CC 4.0)

the border. As a result, they had to operate rather indiscriminately, often jamming Russian communications, too. After the first week, the Russians took to using EW in a much more discriminating way, but this also contributed to the casualty rate among senior officers. The Russian army already had something of a 'leading from the front' ethos, but when colonels and even generals also moved closer to the front line to get a better tactical picture, they also become more vulnerable to snipers and artillery.

Gen. Chaiko's main force of more than 10,000 troops, almost 1,000 tanks and another 2,400 other vehicles, might represent a powerful armoured force in ideal circumstances, but in these conditions posed seemingly insurmountable logistical, technical, and administrative challenges. Ambushes, breakdowns, congestion, incompetence, empty fuel tanks, false alarms, and opportunistic looting expeditions all contributed to turning an ambitious invasion into a 65km traffic jam.

Instead of being at the outskirts of Kyiv by 26 February the main body of the force had by then only reached Ivankiv. While advance parties were able to make better time and launch the aforementioned attacks, their speed was bought at the price of mass and supply, which is one reason why their operations were so often piecemeal and small-scale. By 1 March the column had made only 40km more along the P02, having effectively ground to a halt around Demydiv, some 25km north of the city. In the following days, as if admitting defeat, this column largely dispersed into wooded areas, farms, and other forms of cover, both against enemy attack and the elements. Considering that reconstituting the column would take time and be easily visible to Ukrainian drones and Western satellites, the implication was that even then, its commanders believed they would not be fighting their way into Kyiv. Meanwhile, Gen. Lapin's column to the east had only reached Honcharivske, 15km from the city limits. By 4 March, they had reached and taken Brovary, a suburban town on the east of Kyiv, but would get no further.

The defence of Kyiv

Had the Russians been able to take, hold, and use Antonov Airport as planned to assault into the city centre; had they been able otherwise to break through Hostomel and Bucha quickly to open a way into what was, in the first week, still a largely undefended capital; had they simply been able and willing to revise their plans quickly, encircling it to prevent reinforcement, then Kyiv might have fallen. Instead, though, with the over-optimistic initial plans in ruins, the Russian commanders seemed unable to develop anything new that better matched the situation on the ground.

Kyiv was defended in skirmishes and pitched battles in towns and villages around it – including Hostomel, Bucha, Irpin, Moshchun, and Vorzel, west of Bucha – and around its periphery, as Russian forces delivered not the hammer blow intended but a series of uncoordinated and often limited assaults. By the beginning of March, more troops were being thrown into the defence of the capital, including the 95th Indep

Airborne Bde and the National Guard's 1st and 4th Bdes, as well as elements of the 112th and 114th Territorial Defence Bdes and armed civilian militias. The 43rd and 45th Indep Artillery Bdes provided some long-range counter-battery capability, especially with their massive 203mm 2S7 Pion SPGs.

Meanwhile, Gen. Lapin's force to the northeast was essentially unable to get past Brovary, where it would in due course be engaged also by the National

New Territorial Defence Forces recruits are given basic instruction on the use of an NLAW AT launcher in a public park in Kyiv. (Getty)

THE UKRAINIAN NATIONAL GUARD

The National Guard of Ukraine is a gendarmerie subordinated to the MVS, which since the 2022 invasion has become more and more heavily militarized. It was originally established at the end of 1991, following Ukraine's independence, and while in 2000 it was merged with another force subordinated to the Interior Ministry, the Interior Troops, it was reformed in 2014. The Interior Troops, after all, were associated with the repressions carried out by the former Yanukovych regime, and there was a desperate need to raise more troops in the aftermath of the Crimean annexation and undeclared war in the Donbas. Crucially, it represented a structure which could in due course incorporate the numerous volunteer militias which sprang up to resist local insurgents and their Russian patrons in the Donbas. By the start of 2022, they numbered some 60,000 officers, which would rise to 90,000 after the invasion. Along with local security elements and centrally subordinated units such as the Headquarters Protection & Support Bn,, the National Guard has seven operational brigades (the 1st, 3rd, 4th, 12th, 13th, 14th and 15th), an artillery brigade, and two special forces units, Omega and Typhoon.

Guard's Azov Rgt, a unit infamous for its roots in an ultra-nationalist militia but also known for its combat prowess. Well equipped with Javelins and NLAWs, it was able to prevent an attempted breakthrough by a BTG drawn from the 90th Guards Tank Div. Initially, NLAWs were used to immobilize both lead and rear vehicles, then a Stuhna-P launcher began picking off tanks while artillery rounds began slamming into the Russians as they tried to withdraw. They were routed with heavy losses, including 17 tanks and three other AFVs, and the casualties included their commander, Col. Andrei Zakharov.

Nonetheless, Kyiv suffered, not least by regular artillery strikes that pounded military and civilian targets alike, as well as cruise and ballistic missile strikes from Kalibr (SS-N-30A) and Iskander (SS-26) systems. On 1 March, two missiles hit the Kyiv TV Tower, although most services were quickly rerouted through internet rather than broadcast media. Despite Russia's failure to establish air superiority, the city was also subject to periodic air attacks, losing two of its advanced Su-35S 'Super Flankers' from the 23rd Fighter Aviation Rgt in the process to Ukrainians SAMs.

The Ukrainians strike back

The Ukrainians were not satisfied simply with blocking the Russian advance, not least because, as one British soldier working with them at that early stage noted, 'at some point even Moscow would get its act together.' From mid-March, Kyiv began mustering forces for a counterattack right across the region. This was launched on 22 March, and in many ways finally pushed Moscow into recognizing that it was not going to be taking Kyiv.

The Kalibr family of sea- and air-launched cruise missiles are accurate, hard-hitting, and long-ranged, meaning that even ships from Russia's Black Sea Fleet and Caspian Flotilla could deliver strikes on Kyiv. (Mil.ru, CC 4.0)

Before they would essentially find themselves following the Russian withdrawal, the Ukrainians were able to break the stalemates which had emerged in so many towns in the Kyiv Region. For example, the town of Makaryv, west of the capital, first came under attack on 27 February, by a small Russian column of 15 tanks, 25 APCs, and 15 trucks from a BTG of the 64th Indep Motor Rifle Bde. They were planning just to pass through on their way eastwards, but met fierce local resistance by volunteers, police, and no more than a platoon of troops. This sparked a back-and-forth struggle for the city between the original attackers, later reinforced by another BTG of the 37th Indep Motor Rifle Bde, and a defending force drawn from the Ukrainian 14th Indep Mech Bde and the 95th Air Assault Bde. On 2 March, the defenders claimed to have fully recaptured Makariv, but as late as the 22nd the town's mayor admitted that it was still being contested. In the following days, though, the Ukrainian forces, further reinforced by VTO and National Guard units, were able to push the Russians hard such that they withdrew on 1 April.

Similar small-scale victories were being won across Kyiv and Chernihiv Regions, but in any case, Moscow had had enough. On 25 March, Col. Gen. Sergei Rudskoi, Russia's Deputy Chief of the General Staff and head of the GOU, affirmed that 'in general, the main goals of the first stage of the operation are complete.' Claiming (with a straight face) that for humanitarian reasons, there had never been any intention of assaulting major cities, he added that sufficient damage had been done to Ukraine's military capacities that the Russians could focus on the 'liberation' of the Donbas to the east. This was, of course, a face-saving way of announcing the end of the attempt to take Kyiv, and on 29 March, bending to the realities on the ground, the Russians began withdrawing from the whole region (and, indeed, the neighbouring Sumy region to the west, which had experienced its own abortive attack). Bucha was retaken by the Ukrainians on 1 April, revealing the massacre there. By 6 April, the Russians had completed their retreat from both Kyiv and Chernihiv regions, albeit under steady Ukrainian harassment, in order to concentrate on the eastern Donbas regions, and Odesa and Zaporizhia in the south. In their wake, they left the hundreds of vehicles, destroyed, damaged or simply abandoned, and the bodies of many of their best troops.

RETAKING MAKARYV

Makaryv, 29 March, 2022. Ukrainian forces are pushing the Russians out of the town. A National Guardswoman from the 25th Public Security Protection Brigade, named after Prince Askold, shelters behind an MT-LB APC and reloads her AKM-47, while a regular soldier from the 95th Air Assault Brigade lays down suppressive fire at a building in the city centre still occupied by Russian troops. A Russian BMP-2 from the 37th Independent Motor Rifle Brigade, marked with an 'O' recognition symbol, burns, possibly destroyed by the RPG-22 disposable AT rocket, whose launch tube lies discarded in the foreground. The Russians are still putting up a fight, with a PKM machinegun firing from across the street, but the greatest danger may come from the Orlan-10 reconnaissance drone overflying the street at an unusually low altitude, as this could be feeding live imagery to a nearby artillery command post, although at this early stage of the war, the response times to such spotting could be anything from a few minutes to half an hour.

ANALYSIS

Today I initiated a phone call with the president of the Russian Federation. The result was silence.

    Volodymyr Zelensky, addressing the nation on 23 February 2022

Was this a foolish adventure bound to fail, or a defensible gamble that simply didn't work out? Certainly, this was a dramatic reversal: in the sprawling battles around the outskirts of Kyiv, for example, some 3,000 Ukrainian troops – albeit assisted by thousands of armed civilians, police and militias – drove off some 15,000 Russians. How far was this a failure of planning or execution? On the one hand, the operation's concept was a familiar one. Citing interventions in Czechoslovakia, Afghanistan, Kosovo, and Crimea, Collins, Kofman, and Spenser argue that:

> This high-risk, high-reward strategy was not atypical given the number of such operations in Russian and Soviet history, including Operation Danube in 1968, Storm-333 in 1979, the seizure of Pristina airport in 1999, and the airborne airlift into Simferopol airport during the seizure of Crimea in 2014. If anything, the attempt was stereotypical of prior regime change operations.

When crushing the Prague Spring in Czechoslovakia, while initially deploying a force not that much greater than the defenders' (though it would soon be expanded), the Soviets could rely on deep divisions not only within the Czechoslovak People's Army but also within the national leadership. This does appear to be how Putin envisaged his invasion of Ukraine playing out, too. However, Storm-333, the operation which toppled one leader of Afghanistan and imposed another, on the back of a surgical special forces operation and a massive land invasion, relied on the active support of a substantial faction within the government – and even then led not to victory,

A destroyed T-72 abandoned as the Russians retreated from positions south of Chernihiv on 31 March; note the O recognition sign painted on the remaining sideskirts. (Getty)

but a debilitating ten-year war that the Soviets never managed to win.[4] The 'Pristina Dash' in which Russian paratroopers occupied an airport ahead of NATO forces was a rather different operation, given that both sides were notionally joint peacekeepers, while the seizure of Crimea depended on ideal conditions on the ground.

In other words, one can certainly draw parallels, even if, as with Afghanistan (and the First Chechen War, which likewise began with an attempt to seize the capital, Grozny), these are not always especially encouraging examples. Nonetheless, especially for an invader who believes that the defenders would be divided, demoralized, and disorganized, it might seem reasonable to attempt a *coup de main*, seizing the capital and capturing, killing, or expelling the political leadership to clear the way for imposing a new, compliant one at bayonet point. Of course, in practice many of the political assumptions were deeply flawed, not least that taking Kyiv would have been enough to claim victory. In fact, Putin would as likely have reprised Napoleon's experience after his capture of Moscow in 1812, as he was left impatiently waiting for a Russian surrender that would not be forthcoming.

Never say never, though: it is noteworthy that even the best Western defence analysts, including those privy to intelligence assessments, believed that Russia would win, and probably do so in a matter of weeks or at most months. Thus, it is impossible to say that the invasion was bound to fail. However, it is possible to highlight some of the factors which ultimately ensured the Russians were forced to revise their whole plan of campaign.

1. Unrealistic expectations

There is no doubt that Putin's prejudices about Ukraine crucially shaped many of the bases of the operation. In this, one could almost describe him

---

4   See RAID 54, *Storm-333. KGB and Spetsnaz seize Kabul, Soviet–Afghan War 1979*

A destroyed block of flats in Borodyanka, northeast of Kyiv. (Getty)

as Ukraine's secret weapon. He had, over more than two decades of direct and indirect rule, created a system in which no one would dare contradict him. As an alleged FSB analyst admitted in a leaked letter, the culture was that 'you have to write the analysis in a way that makes Russia the victor... otherwise you get questioned for not doing good work.' Arrogance and self-deception are a dangerous combination. As Ukraine's Gen. Zaluzhny later put it,

> A failure to fear resistance, an inability to imagine that someone can hit and destroy the second most powerful army in the world – it had drawn to Kyiv these convoys that we ended up burning down.

2. Inadequate preparation

One consequence of those unrealistic expectations was that the invading force was inadequately prepared. Without mobilization or the capacity to use conscripts (whose deployment would have been politically explosive), its BTGs were often short of infantry, so elite units such as *Spetsnaz* and paratroopers were thrown into battle as light infantry and took catastrophic losses. The initial MRAU strike was less extensive than it ought to have been, and frequently based on dated intelligence, also contributing to their failure to achieve air superiority. More generally, the Russians had to rely on an ultimately fruitless dash

for Kyiv instead of a campaign fought the way they were trained and armed to fight. As Watling, Danylyuk, and Reynolds put it:

> The Russian motor rifle and Rosgvardia troops had received their orders less than 24 hours before the invasion. As a consequence, they did not fight a methodical campaign of breakthrough and exploitation by successive echelons as their doctrine dictated, nor were they supported by sufficient artillery as is considered essential. Instead, they were pushed forwards along two main resupply routes (MSRs) towards distant objectives without reconnaissance or screening to their flanks.

The T-72B3 was the backbone of Russia's armoured forces, and although many were destroyed, like this one abandoned outside Mariupol (hence the Z recognition symbol), it has proven a surprisingly effective modernization of an ageing design. (Mvs.gov.ua, CC 4.0)

3. Morale

The lack of a proper build-up to the invasion also extended to preparing the Russian troops for war psychologically. The Ukrainians knew they were fighting for their sovereignty and the very survival of their nation, and in effect had been getting ready ever since the annexation of Crimea in 2014. The Russians – many of whom still regarded the Ukrainians as their cousins – had largely assumed they were simply on exercises, and were at best only partially convinced by Putin's claims of a threat from a 'Nazi' Kyiv. Indeed, as one Russian officer, invalided out of service, bitterly framed it, 'we were told we were like the heroes of the Great Patriotic War [World War II], when really we felt like we were the Nazi-fascists.'

The Russians failed to learn many of the lessons they learned so bitterly during the two Chechen wars. In this image from the first war, two Russian IFVs, knocked out by grenades when deployed without infantry cover, lie abandoned on a main street in Grozny. (Getty)

This contributed both to their uncharacteristic unwillingness to take casualties in the name of accomplishing their objectives, but also the rampant indiscipline in the ranks. The regular army, at least, had initially been instructed to treat the Ukrainians decently, but the opportunities for looting, fear metastasizing into anger, and poor command skills on the part of often-inexperienced junior officers all combined to terrible effect. Besides which, the Rosgvardiya (and especially the Kadyrovtsy) had from the beginning been tasked with rounding up potential and presumed troublemakers in the local population, and this all too quickly became licence to bully, beat and even kill.

4. Urban war

The Russian forces were trained and equipped primarily for fast-moving combined arms manoeuvre warfare. Having failed to secure a quick win, they faced a determined enemy in dense urban environments, where many of their advantages were nullified or actively proved disadvantages. Armoured units sent in without adequate infantry cover were decimated by AT systems or simply well-aimed Molotov cocktails thrown onto the engine intakes on their rear decks. Lightly armed paratrooper detachments were deployed as if they were heavy mechanized forces and suffered the consequences. Rosgvardiya units trained in riot control found themselves fighting a determined, well-armed military. In due course, the Russians would adopt an approach akin to the one they adopted in retaking the Chechen capital Grozny, reducing urban strongholds through massive long-range bombardment, followed by a methodical, block-by-block

clearance. In the early stages of the war, though, the Russians too often tried to rush urban settlements, only to find themselves forced back by determined and dug-in enemies, forewarned of their approach by drones or simply civilian spotters.

5. Logistics

It is easy to believe that Putin and his cronies, whose background was in the Soviet KGB rather than the military, committed the classic amateur's mistake of neglecting 'tail' – logistics – for 'teeth.' The assumption that Russia's forces would either have won in a few days, or at least would have reached secure locations in which they could be resupplied, proved a catastrophic misjudgement. Soldiers were forced to loot for supplies, which both undermined discipline and further alienated the locals, vehicles had to be abandoned when they ran out of fuel, and assaults were delayed for lack of ammunition. Narrow supply lines were vulnerable to direct attacks or denial through blowing dams and bridges, mining roads, and blocking bottlenecks. Besides, Russian forces tend to rely heavily on non-palletized bulk supply by rail, and railway lines were especially vulnerable, as well as the key depots and distribution points. None of these were insurmountable obstacles, but they are precisely the kind of detailed preparatory work that

A Russian supply truck, marked with both the infamous Z and 'Dagestan' – presumably where the driver is from – drives through the occupied part of Izyum. Frontline resupply was a constant problem for the invaders. (Getty)

73

The forces of the former pseudo-states of Donetsk and Lugansk could fight bravely, but as often proved recalcitrant, abusive, and resentful of their new role as Moscow's cannon fodder. Here, two DNR soldiers in mismatched equipment and white recognition tape walk towards the frontline in the port city of Mariupol, where they would take heavy losses. (Getty)

the General Staff's GOU and NTsUO are there for, and neither was properly involved beforehand.

6. Corruption

The Russian military had looked very impressive when on parade, and twenty years of a high-spending modernization programme were meant to have created a modern and capable force. In part, this was undoubtedly true, but when tested in a major war, it quickly became clear that the corruption at the heart of Putin's system had also eaten away at military capabilities. Supposedly secure radios proved to be based on insecure Chinese civilian models; supply trucks were fitted with cheap civilian tyres instead of the rugged all-terrain ones intended; all too many ration packs were out-of-date ones simply put into new boxes; the list of such incidents is a long and shabby one.

7. Command and control

At first, there was a glaring lack of coordination between army groups and fronts, each having their own commander and competing for scarce resources. Only on 10 April was a single overall commander for the SVO appointed, Gen. Alexander Dvornikov. Even so, he was the army commander, and the National Guard forces in-theatre, to say nothing of the Kadyrovtsy and later the Wagner mercenaries, often regarded his orders as little more than suggestions. One of the reasons why Kadyrov would later fall out with Gen. Lapin, for example, was his desire to see the Chechen troops play a more aggressive role at the front rather than simply looting and killing civilians in the rear. Col. Daniil Martynov, the commander of the Kadyrovtsy in-theatre, nonetheless would ostentatiously refer all orders Lapin gave him to Grozny to be cleared. Furthermore, the forces of the former DNR and LNR (which would formally become the 1st Donetsk Army Corps and 2nd Guards Luhansk-Sievierodonetsk Army Corps) were heavily manned by pressganged recruits, corrupt even by the standards of the Russian military, and often officered by men who resented now being put under regulars, all of which compounded these challenges.

Command and control problems ran all the way down. While the Russian and Soviet military had always prioritized obedience over initiative, in recent years a serious effort had been made to address this. Nonetheless, this was still a work in progress, and all too often Russian commanders would find it hard to show initiative when they had little sense of what their superiors actually wanted, and how their small part of the SVO fit into the wider plan. In part, this was a result of, again, the lack of warning and preparation, in part communication difficulties, and in part because of how quickly the overall plan fell apart in the face of realities on the ground. Either way, this led to some cases in which units ran far ahead of the rest of the advance and were left isolated and vulnerable, but more often led to a cautious, even hesitant approach. It also contributed to the fratricidal 'friendly fire' incidents which so dogged the Russians (indeed, in the first two years of the war alone, at least 13 of their military aircraft were downed by their own air defences).

CONCLUSION

The war is started by career soldiers, and finished by teachers, engineers, accountants.

Gen. Valery Zaluzhny

The overall failure of the initial Russian invasion – of which the battle for Kyiv was only one front – was not just the opening stage of a war, it was also a curtain-raiser for a new style of war altogether. Of course, the continuities such as the evergreen importance of artillery and the way the Poor Bloody Infantry are still essential for holding territory, tend to be overshadowed by the novelties. Nonetheless, this war, as it has evolved, has indeed showcased some of the evolving trends of conflict in the twenty-first century.

Of course, the most evident has been the rise of the drone, and while the Ukrainians may have been the first to appreciate its true value, the Russians have been close behind. Within a couple of years, drones would become a central element of this war, allowing both sides a clear tactical picture within at least 10 km of the line of contact – and what you can see, you can generally

THE ZALA LANCET

Produced by ZALA, a subsidiary of the Russian Kalashnikov arms combine, the Lancet is a highly capable loitering munition, essentially a drone missile which can either be used for reconnaissance or be smashed into a target with a high-explosive, thermobaric, or AT shaped-charge warhead. Launched from a simple ground- or ship-mounted catapult, it can fly at up to 100km/h, has a range of 40km, and can stay in the air for 30 minutes (although more advanced versions have up to an hour's endurance). A single Lancet is unlikely to destroy a modern tank, but independent assessments of their effectiveness in Ukraine suggest they destroy almost a third of their targets and seriously damage as many again, which helps explain why one Ukrainian officer told a meeting in London that 'the Lancet is the single most dangerous weapon in the Russian arsenal.'

hit – and becoming terrors of both frontline troops and cities and supply depots far to the rear. Even in the early days and weeks of the invasion, they were emerging as a crucial force multiplier, especially for the defence, and also one generated often from commercial and 'garage industry' sources, as Ukrainian civilians would use their own recreational drones for spotting, often buying them for the very purpose or assembling them in their garages and kitchens.

A Ukrainian Bayraktar TB2 drone, with two ground control stations in the background, surprised friends and foes alike in the early stages of the war, providing the Ukrainians with an invaluable reconnaissance capability. (armyinform.com. ua, CC 4.0)

Once, the notion of a 'people's war' was framed in terms of mobilization a substantial proportion of the population being used to fight or dig trenches. In Ukraine, it manifested not just in civilians helping fortify Kyiv, stacking tyres at Mykolaiv street junctions to be lit as an early warning beacon, or building drones, but also acting as the army's eyes and ears generally. Social media in particular began to be used to pass on alerts about troop movements, aircraft flying overhead, and gunfire heard in the distance. The OSINT (Open Source Intelligence) provided through the analysis of generally available information and images even become a globally crowdsourced process, as experts and amateurs around the world digested and commented on it. Much, of course, was obvious, credulous, or downright wrong, but there was nonetheless gold amidst the dross. One HUR officer described how a group of foreign OSINT amateurs nonetheless gave them the first warnings that the Russians were moving advanced S-400 AA missiles forward to protect the 'Kyiv convoy' from potential Ukrainian attack, from creative analysis of blurred social media posts.

After all, in a truly global information space, the Ukrainians also quickly came to appreciate the importance of global fund-raising, cheerleading, and even recruitment to their International Legion. First, the far-flung Ukrainian diaspora (especially in Canada) rallied to their cause, then other allies, who lobbied their governments to provide aid, and highlighted Kyiv's successes and Moscow's failures and abuses alike. They also became platforms for fundraising efforts of their own. Much of this was for individual-scale assistance such as body armour, medical kits, and second-hand SUVs for mobility, but in 2022, Czechs would raise the money to buy and donate a modernized T-72 ('Tomaš the Tank') and Lithuanians for a Bayraktar TB2 drone. While dwarfed by the levels of assistance that would in due course be provided by Western governments, these flows of resources and equipment were often more timely and also had a powerful effect on morale within the country. Indeed, the extent to which grass-roots international support for the Ukrainians' cause could affect the battlefield was also evident when Belarusians opposed to the authoritarian regime of President Lukashenko actively sabotaged rail lines used by the Russians for resupply.

The bloodily-learned lessons would keep coming, though. For the Ukrainians, this is a war for the very survival of their nation, while Putin has sought to wrap his imperial adventure in the mantle of the Great Patriotic War, dragging everyone from historians to priests into this venture. On 3 April 2022,

At the regular Victory Day parade in Moscow on 9 May, 2022, flags of the DNR and LNR were flown and Putin drew direct comparisons between this war and the defence of the Motherland from invaders, from the Poles in the 17th century to the Nazis in the 20th. The unsubtle subtext was that this was a war that was only just starting, and which Russia could not afford to lose. (Getty)

Patriarch Kirill, head of the Russian Orthodox Church, gave a sermon at the gold-and-khaki Cathedral of the Armed Forces outside Moscow, pledging that 'we have broken the back of fascism once; we will do it again.' Nonetheless, the failed attack on Kyiv proved just the start of the bloodiest war in Europe since 1945, that would see both Ukraine and Russia suffering terrible losses yet without (as of writing) either side being able to break the other.

'RAIL WAR' IN BELARUS

One contentious topic is the degree to which sabotage in Belarus, especially of the railway system used to transport men and materiel, undermined the initial invasion effort. Later in the war, the Ukrainian intelligence agencies and Russians hostile to the war and the regime would carry out sabotage in Russia itself, but very soon after the start of the invasion, reports began to surface about attacks in Belarus, one of the key staging posts for the operation. Autocratic Belarusian president Alexander Lukashenko was, after all, having to balance placating his only real ally and patron, Putin, while retaining his autonomy and not risking sparking renewed protest at home. The compromise was therefore that Russia would have free rein of Belarusian soil to prepare and stage the invasion, and later also access to Belarusian arsenals when ammunition stocks were running low, but that no Belarusian troops would take part. There were locals opposed both to the invasion and Lukashenko's regime, and very soon they began a small-scale but still significant campaign of railway sabotage.

Typically, this entailed setting fire to signalling equipment and relay cabinets, something that can be done relatively safely and yet which will either force a stop on train traffic or at least slow them down to around 15km/h. More sophisticated attacks were carried out either by railway workers or else hackers attacking the system of BCh, the state railway company. Even according to official figures, at least 80 acts of sabotage had been carried out by mid-April 2022. The result was episodic disruption, problematic and embarrassing enough that in March, Deputy Interior Minister Gennady Kazakevich threatened that saboteurs could be shot on sight, and in April, the Belarusian legislature passed a law to allow the use of the death penalty for sabotage. All told, several hundred people were involved in a campaign which also saw at least two injured by gunfire when caught by the security forces. The campaign petered out as Russia shifted its war effort to the east and south, but nonetheless emphasized the degree to which even in authoritarian regimes, resistance endures.

FURTHER READING

Collins, Liam, Michael Kofman and John Spencer. 'The Battle of Hostomel Airport: A Key Moment in Russia's Defeat in Kyiv,' *War On The Rocks*, 10 August 2023

Cooper, Tom et al. *War in Ukraine, Volume 2: Russian invasion, February 2022* (Helion, 2023)

Galeotti, Mark. *Forged in War. A military history of Russia from its beginnings to today* (Osprey, 2024)

Harrel, John. *The Russian Invasion of Ukraine, February–December 2022: destroying the myth of Russian invincibility* (Pen & Sword, 2023)

Lawrence, Christopher. *The Battle for Kyiv. The fight for Ukraine's capital* (Frontline, 2023)

Matthews, Owen. *Overreach: the inside story of Putin and Russia's war against Ukraine* (Mudlark, 2022)

Miller, Christopher. *The War Came to Us. Life and death in Ukraine* (Bloomsbury, 2023)

Ryan, Mick. *The War for Ukraine. Strategy and adaptation under fire* (Naval Institute Press, 2024)

Sladden, James, Liam Collins and Ben Connable. 'The Battle of Irpin River,' *British Army Review*, Spring 2024

Trofimov, Yaroslav. *Our Enemies Will Vanish* (Michael Joseph, 2024)

Watling, Jack and Nick Reynolds. 'Operation Z: The Death Throes of an Imperial Delusion,' *RUSI Special Report* (2022)

Watling, Jack, Oleksandr Danylyuk and Nick Reynolds. 'Preliminary Lessons from Russia's Unconventional Operations During the Russo-Ukrainian War, February 2022–February 2023,' *RUSI Special Report* (2023)

INDEX

Figures in **bold** refer to illustrations.

agents within Ukrainian forces 17–18
aircraft: Antonov An-225 21; Ilyushin Il-76 20; Kamov-52 helicopter 20, **20**, **34–35** (33); MiG-29 29; Mil Mi-8 helicopter **14**, 20, 33, **34–35** (33); Mil Mi-24 helicopter 20, 33, **34–35** (33); Su-25 Grach **43**; Sukhoi Su-24 33, 48; Sukhoi Su-34 'Fullback' 48; Sukhoi Su-35 'Super Flanker' **29**, 64
atrocities 44
Atroshenko, Vladyslav (mayor of Chernihiv) 49

Bartosh, Col. Alexander 8–9
Belarus **9**, 21, 29, 32–33
Beseda, Col. Gen. Sergei 7, 11
bombs 48
Borodyanka 70
Bortnikov, Alexander (Russian Security Service Director) 11
bridges, pontoon 48, 54–55
Bucha 40–44, 65
Budanov, Lt. Gen. Kyrylo 9
Burns, William (CIA Director) 9

Chaiko, Col. Gen. Alexander 21, 62
Chechen Wars 69, **72**
Chernihiv 45–49
Chernobyl Nuclear Power Plant 21, 36
command and control failings 74–75
corruption 74
Crimea 4–5
cyber attacks 24

Debaltseve, Donbas **6**
Deineko, Lt. Gen. Serhii 26
Demydiv 53–54
Donbas region 5–6
Donetsk, 'people's republic' of (DNR) 5–6, 13, **74**, 75, **78**
drones 24–26, 61, **66–67** (65), 76–77, **77**
Dvornikov, Gen. Alexander 74

electronic warfare (EW) **17**, 61–62
European Union (EU), Association Agreement with the 4

Fastiv 55
Federal Security Service (FSB), Russian: 5th Service 7, 12
friendly fire 39, 75

Gerasimov, Gen. Valery 7, **7**, 12

Horenka 50, 56–57
Hostomel (Antonov) Airport, Kyiv 20, 29–40, **30**, **33**, **34–35** (33)

invasion: plan 7–8; begins 14–17, 26–27; extent **22**
Irpin 55–60, **60**
Irpin River 37, 53–57
Ivankiv 36, 45, 62
Izyum 73

Kadyrov, Ramzan 18, 74–75
Kharkiv, Ukraine 23
Kherson, Ukraine 23
Khoda, Col. Leonid 46
Kireyev, Denys 9
Kirill, Patriarch 78
Kolokoltsev, Vladimir (Russian Interior Minister) 13
Kolychivka 48
Kovalchuk, Yuri 7, 11
Kozak, Dmitry (deputy head Russian Presidential Administration) 13
Kozarovychi (Irpin) Dam 53
Krasukha-2 EW system **17**
Kryvoruchko, Gen. Serhii 17

Lapin, Gen. Alexander 21, **23**, 62–65, 75
Lavrov, Sergei (Russian Foreign Minister) 11
logistics 73–74
Lugansk, 'people's republic' of (LNR) 5–6, 13, 75, **78**

Macron, President Emmanuel 11
Main Intelligence Directorate (GU), Russian 18, 27
Main Operations Directorate (GOU), Russian 7, 16
Makaryv **66–67** (65)
Mariupol 23, **71**, **74**
markings, tactical **5**, 21
Markushyn, Oleksandr (mayor of Irpin) 57
Martynov, Col. Daniil 75
Massed Missile-Aviation Strike (MRAU) 17
Medvedchuk, Viktor 11–12, 23
Molotov cocktails 41–42
morale 71–72
Moschun 57
Mykolaiv, Ukraine 23

Naryshkin, Sergei (head of Russian SVR) 12–13
National Defence Management Centre (NTsUO) **16**, 16–17
NATO 8, 10
Novi Yarylovychi 25

Omurbekov, Col. Azatbek 41, 44
Open Source Intelligence (OSINT) 77
Organization for Security and Cooperation in Europe 10
Osokin, Maj. Alexei 38

Pankov, Col. Vadim 20, 32
Pasechnik, Leonid (head of LNR) 13
Patrushev, Nikolai (Russian Security Council Secretary) 11, **11**
protests since 2013 4–5
Pushilin, Denis (head of DNR) 13
Putin, President Vladimir 7; attempts to unsettle Ukraine 4–6; fears Ukraine's NATO membership 4, 8; 'On the Historical Unity of Russians and Ukrainians' 8; places demands on NATO 9–10; receives advisors' opinions 11–13; announces 'Special Military Operation' (SVO) 14; prejudices about Ukraine 69–70

recognition symbols **5**, **33**, **45**, **66–67** (65), **69**, **71**, **73**
recruitment, Ukrainian 10
Redut mercenary army 27
Revolution of Dignity 4
Reznikov, Oleksii (Ukrainian Defence Minister) 24, 40
Rudskoi, Col. Gen. Sergei 65
Russian forces: Central Military District 21; Eastern Military District 21; 2nd Guards Army 21; 5th Combined Arms Army 21; 29th Combined Arms Army 21; 35th Combined Arms Army 21, 36, 41; 36th Combined Arms Army 21; 41st Combined Arms Army 21; 4th Indep Motor Rifle Bde 56; 11th Indep Guards Air Assault Bde 20, 33; 30th Artillery Bde 57; 35th Indep Guards Motor Rifle Bde 47; 37th Indep Motor Rifle Bde 65; 45th Guards *Spetsnaz* Bde 20; 55th Guards Mountain Motor Rifle Bde 47–48; 64th Indep Guards Motor Rifle Bde 41; 74th Indep Guards Motor Rifle Bde 47; 76th Guards Air Assault Div 20, 43; 2nd Bomber Aviation Rgt 48; 23rd Fighter Aviation Rgt 64; 141st Special Motorized Rgt 37, 37–38; 234th Guards Air Assault Rgt 41; 237th Guards Airborne Assault Rgt 37; 331st Guards Airborne Rgt 43; 899th Assault Aviation Rgt 43; 173rd Indep Guards Recon Bn 57; 249th Indep Special Motorized Bn 41; Battalion Tactical Group 5; Chechen gunmen 18–20, **37**, 44; *Kadyrovtsy* gunmen 18–20, **37**, 39, 41, 74; *Rosgvardiya* (National Guard) 16, 21, **52**, 53; Special Rapid-Response Detachment (SOBR) 41; *Spetsnaz* (special forces) 18, **19** (18); Wagner Group mercenary army 27

sabotage, railway 78
Sadokhin, Col. Ihor 17
St. George Cathedral, Lviv **12**
Sanchik, Lt. Gen. Alexander 36
Scholz, Chancellor Olaf 11
Sea Breeze 2019, Exercise **14**
Security Service of Ukraine (SBU) **12**, 18, **26**, 28
Shoigu, Sergei (Russian Defence Minister) 7, **7**, 12
snipers **42**
Soyuznaya Reshimost (Allied Resolve) military exercises 10
'Special Military Operation' (SVO) **14**, 17–18
spending, defence (Ukrainian) 23
Storm-333 (Afghanistan) 68–69
Sukhovetsky, Maj. Gen. Andrei 39
Sumy, Ukraine 23
Syrsky, Col. Gen. Oleksandr 53–54

traffic jam, invasion **45**, 61–62
Tushayev, Lt. Col. Magomed 38

Ukrainian forces: Special Operations Forces Command 24; 1st 'Burevii' Bde **43**, 63; 1st Tank Bde **46**; 4th Op Bde 29, 63; 4th 'Rubizh' Bde 41; 14th Indep Mech Bde 65; 40th Tactical Aviation Bde 29; 43rd Indep Artillery Bde 63; 45th Indep Artillery Bde 63; 58th Motorised Bde 47–48; 72nd Mech Bde 24, 33, 49–52, **51**, 55–56; 95th Air Assault Bde 65; 112th Territorial Defence Bde 25, 63; 114th Territorial Defence Bde 47, 63; Khyzhak Bde (Tactical-Operational Response Team) **28**; 1st Special Purpose Police Assault Rgt 57; 3rd Indep Special Operations Rgt 32; 383rd Indep Unmanned Aviation Complexes Rgt 61; Azov Rgt 15, **16**, 43, 64; 1st Nuclear Power Plant Defence Bn 36, **37**; 208th Territorial Defence Bn 55; 'Shaman' Special Operations Bn 33, **36**; National Guard 63; Territorial Defence Forces (VTO) 24
Ukrainian Military Intelligence (HUR) 9, 33

Vdovychenko, Col. Oleksandr 33, 52
vehicles: BMD 38; BMP-2 IFV **9**, **23**, **45**, **66–67** (65); BTR-60PB **39**, 56; KamAZ-435029 Patrul-A **52**; MT-LB APC **66–67** (65); T-64BM Bulat tank **46**, **47**; T-72 tank **13**, **71**; T-80BVM tank **40**, **45**
Verkhovna Rada (Ukraine parliament) 6
Vostok 2022 strategic command post exercise **7**

weapons: 2S1 Gvozdika howitzer **51**; 2S7 Pion self-propelled howitzer 54, **54**, 63; 2S19 Msta-S self-propelled howitzer 57; BM-27 Uragan (Hurricane) **49**; Dragunov SVD rifle **42**; FGM-148 Javelin anti-tank missile 25, **25**, 55, 61; Kalibr cruise missiles **64**; M4-WAC-47 rifle **26**; NLAW anti-tank weapon 25, 46, 61, **63**; Stinger MANPADS **25**, 29; Stuhna-P missile launcher **46**, **48**, 61; Uragan MLRS 57; ZALA Lancet loitering munition 56, 76; Zbroyar Z-008 rifle **42**; ZU-23-2 AA gun **31**
withdrawal from Kyiv, Russian 65

Yahidne 48
Yanukovych, President Viktor 4

Zakharov, Col. Andrei 64
Zelensky, President Volodymyr **18**, 20; assassination attempt **19** (18), 27–28; at Munich Security Conference 10
Zolotov, Gen. Viktor 13, **14**